MW01698105

The Road to Oman:
The Journey of Hockey Jamaica to the Inaugural Hockey5s World Cup 2024

Sports Administration Insights and Lessons

Fabian Stewart

"A journey of a thousand miles begins with a single step."
- Lao Tzo

I do hope you will enjoy reading about my steps to Jamaica's historical Journey to Oman

2024

ISBN 978 976 97438 0 9

Table of Contents

List of Figures

List of Tables

ABBREVIATIONS

FIH - Fédération Internationale de Hockey (International Hockey Federation)
IF - International Federation (Continental)
IOC - International Olympic Committee
JHF - Jamaica Hockey Federation
JOA - Jamaica Olympic Association
KPI - Key Performance Indicators
LOC - Local Organizing Committee
NOC - National Olympic Committee
PAHF - Pan American Hockey Federation
SDF - Sports Development Foundation
TTO - Trinidad and Tobago
PASO - Pan American Sports Organization
TMS - Tournament Management System

Marjorie Hibbert
1944 - 2024

Dedication

I dedicate this book to my dear mother, Marjorie Hibbert, 'Aunty Madge' to many, who despite only seeing me play one, possibly two, field hockey games in person, was well informed of all my exploits in all my sporting endeavours from school to junior and senior national representation. I probably owe what some regard as my unique mental toughness and dogged determination, a prerequisite of sports management in the Caribbean, to the role she played as the 'mother who fathered me' due to the untimely death of my father, Anthony Stewart, in 1983 when I was only eleven years old.

Her battle with cancer started in 1992 and would include a mastectomy and multiple bouts of treatment following several recurrences and then remission until her passing on Thursday, July 4, 2024. She was 79 years old and her fight with cancer was nothing less than remarkable.

Her steadfast faith and resolve allowed her to keep positively moving forward from the depths of despair – a breadwinner murdered in September 1984 while she was a stay-at-home mother tending to four children. In order to help us emerge from the socioeconomic and financial challenges, she undertook two physically demanding jobs to support the family while ensuring that all our nutritional and scholastic needs were met without compromise. There were few complaints, even as the weariness of the fight with cancer was evident. I can still hear her encouraging us to trust God, to solve our challenges and keep moving forward in faith.

Her life example is the foundation on which my personal life and leadership philosophy are built. Being a part of her life's journey and witnessing this uncompromising resilience and attitude of never giving up, no matter how daunting your circumstances, by staring down your fears in faith and pushing forward, are the tenets of my philosophy.

I would also like to thank my wife, Rose, and our son, Diallo, as well as my close friends and family for their understanding of the demands on my time and resources which were required to serve the interest of the Jamaica Hockey Federation (JHF) for over eight years as its President, as well as my tenure on the Jamaica Olympic Association (JOA) and the Pan American Hockey Federation (PAHF) boards.

Diallo and Rose Lemonius-Stewart

Acknowledgements

The crafting of The Road to Oman is about the accomplishments of a team of individuals and stakeholders at the Jamaica Hockey Federation (JHF) who believed in the need for change in order to begin to realize the potential of the sport and the organization. Therefore, I must acknowledge the members of my functional–dysfunctional hockey family for allowing and supporting my leadership for the past eight consecutive years, starting in 2016.

It would be remiss of me not to thank Dr. Michelle Holt, Michael Blair, Audrey Gaynor, Victor Tomlinson and Dr. Sharmella Roopchand-Martin from the Faculty of Sport, UWI Academy of Sport, for the roles they each played in making this journey a reality. I also do not believe my stewardship of the Federation, nor our historic accomplishment, would have been possible without the tremendous support of Dr. Carlton Campbell. Dr. Campbell's work as a JHF Director responsible for infrastructure, his keen business acumen, counsel and friendship provided a foundation for the Road to Oman, hence this book.

The support of Alberto 'Coco' Budeisky, President of the Pan American Hockey Federation (PAHF) and his team, particularly Laura Marchiotti, has been outstanding through to the completion of this book. Tayyab Ikram, President, Fédération Internationale de Hockey/International Hockey Federation (FIH), must also be acknowledged for his support of the JHF's efforts along the Road to Oman.

The Honourable Olivia 'Babsy' Grange MP, CD, Minister of Sport, and Christopher Samuda, President of the Jamaica Olympic Association (JOA), must be acknowledged for the tremendous belief, commitment, and financial support provided to the

JHF, especially over the Road to Oman. Despite our vociferous negotiations and appeals for additional funding, their support for hosting the Hockey5s Pan Am World Cup Qualifiers in 2023 and the team's participation in Oman did not waver.

A significant portion of the drafting and research for this book was done in the cool climate of Bryce, Manchester, on the balcony of a house belonging to Pauline Lemonius. Pauline's welcoming spirit and hospitality, coupled with the panoramic view of the surrounding valleys and mountains, shrouded in fog or mist at times, made for an excellent atmosphere for me to write.

My heartfelt gratitude must also be extended to Charmaine McKenzie, Nadine Buckland and Yvette Haughton, editor, commenter, and copywriter, who assisted with the appropriate compilation of this, my first book. Their work, guidance and advice created the essential floor plans for documenting our historic journey along the Road to Oman.

I am deeply grateful to my many friends (Rumpanions) and family members, particularly my wife, Rose, and son, Diallo, who have endured the highs and lows of the sports administration and leadership journey, and supported the mission, where necessary, with invaluable contributions to our effort along the Road to Oman.

Introduction

This book provides a unique perspective on the history-making Road to Oman, the theme for Jamaica's first participation in a field hockey FIH World Cup tournament (Hockey5S) since the British regiment introduced the sport to Jamaica some 120 years ago.

The author uses his travel to Oman, embarked on before the Jamaican contingent, as the background to recount Hockey Jamaica's journey to Oman. This is done by highlighting the easily recognized and critical unseen and unheralded sports management activities that helped to form the foundation upon which Jamaica's Men's team qualified for and subsequently participated in the FIH Hockey5s World Cup held in Muscat, Oman, January 24–31, 2024.

"Hockey5s is the shorter and faster variant of traditional field hockey where each team plays with five players. It is similar to what T20 is to cricket, Rugby7s is to rugby, and 3x3 basketball is to basketball. Hockey5s was first introduced in 2013 with the intent of driving up viewership of hockey by making it quicker, simpler and more entertaining" - (Utathya Nag, 2022).

The sporting arena in the English-speaking Caribbean is unique in terms of the strategies required for leading in the socioeconomic and demographic environment of a former British colony where marketing, finance, career path and social influence are significant factors to be confronted.

These factors make leading or managing a Caribbean sports organization, especially a national federation, extremely difficult.

Therefore, in order to align the stakeholders' values towards desired or shared goals, leaders require an understanding of the complexities of the particular organization, the difficulties posed by the environment and the situation.

This book will share the author's field hockey leadership journey, along with various experiences and lessons obtained from the requisite leadership/management manoeuvrings to lead team Jamaica to its inaugural historic qualification for the FIH Hockey5s World Cup. It highlights and reviews the perspectives of other leaders to uncover critical topics required for effectively running a Caribbean sports federation. Utilizing Contingency (Fiedler 1963) and Situational (Hersey and Blanchard 1970) theories of leadership in a practical manner, the book provides insights on solutions adopted to address the challenges faced within the Jamaican sporting arena, as well as within other small island nation states. Some of the lessons centre around the use of an integrated multidimensional leadership style[1], and the management of fear and risk based on situational knowledge and expeditious, instinctive decision-making – Blink. However, most important, it also provides the use of an appropriate strategic planning process to prioritize objectives and use of the necessary grit to usher in change in our management style, called the Paradigm Shift.

Service in the fields of academics and administration have afforded him the opportunity to evaluate and provide solutions to assist in the overall development of the JHF. In addition, serving across the wide spectrum of the sport in various leadership capacities from playing to administration for the past 40+ years, in school, college, club, and country, has deepened his understanding of the challenges and helped him formulate solutions that aided Hockey Jamaica's recent historical achievement of reaching Oman.

---

1 Andrew Hede, "Integrated Leadership: Multiple Styles for Maximal Effectiveness", in: K.W. Parry (Ed.) *Leadership in the Antipodes: Findings, Implications and a Leader Profile* (Wellington NZ: Victoria University Institute of Policy Studies and the Centre for the Study of Leadership, 2001).

In conjunction with the author's purpose of documenting the history created by Jamaica's Men's field hockey journey to its first FIH World Cup event, it is hoped that by sharing lessons and insights from the experiences, it may assist other

Caribbean sports management administrators and stakeholders with meaningful strategies for the complex problems and challenges faced in the sporting arena of small island nations and developing countries.

The layout of the book follows a simple construct. First reviewing the prerequisites for the development of the journey to Oman – the change management strategies which were put in place upon the author's election as President of the Jamaica Hockey Federation in November 2016. It then chronicles the critical strategic path, based on the strategic planning process that was undertaken for the road to, and finally reaching the tournament in Muscat, Oman. Finally, critical lessons learned along the journey are outlined.

Part I reviews the foundation for the journey of the Jamaican hockey team to Oman, covering the significant historical context of the achievement for the JHF and the key stakeholders involved in shaping and making the journey a reality. Chapter One outlines the historical context within which Jamaica earned its place to the Hockey5s World Cup in Muscat, Oman, and the inspiring and key people upon whose shoulders the journey to Oman can be directly rested. Chapter 2 outlines how the fortuitous plans of the JHF materialized with a new direction, starting with a unique leadership philosophy; critical partnerships; and the development of the Youth Development Program.

PART II highlights the importance of strategic management in the JHF and the effectiveness of leadership in the strategic management planning process of building the foundation for the journey to Oman. It reviews the planning process in the unique sports management environment and the introduction of change management thinking (the Paradigm Shift). The highlighting of aspects of the key strategic objectives or pillars, such as a major tournament and national team excellence, will provide insights into the genesis of the Elite Coaching Program, the journey through the COVID-19 pandemic, the final suspension of the restrictions and how the JHF facilitated participation in regional competitions enroute to qualification for the World Cup in Oman.

Part III outlines aspects of event management in sport with a look at the important planning for the Pan American Hockey 5s World Cup Qualifying tournament in Jamaica and its execution. The major milestone reached was becoming the first country to host a qualification tournament for the Hockey5s World Cup in the Pan Am region. The Rocky Road to Oman after the team's qualification precedes the Experience in Oman at the Championship.

The book concludes by reiterating or identifying the major lessons learned along this Road to Oman. While not recommending a fit for all circumstances, the book unearths serious challenges in our Caribbean and/or small island sporting environments and addresses potential solutions for success.

I encourage you to read this entertaining perspective on a sport's journey in history to understand, compare and contrast and continue to add to your knowledge on the management of sports, especially in small island states.

PART I:
The Foundation of the Road to Oman

Part I of this book introduces the historical context and significance of Jamaica's participation in the inaugural FIH Hockey5s World Cup tournament in Muscat, Oman. It highlights the key people in the foundation, development, and culmination of a six-year journey to participate in Oman while referencing relevant leadership philosophies such as Contingency theory (Fiedler 1963) and Situational theory (Hersey and Blanchard 1970). We also review the technical partnerships and the development of the youth program that formed the basis of the journey to Oman.

Acting as the forward management team of one for the Jamaican contingent, the 24+-hour earlier departure of the author and Head of Delegation to Muscat is used as the staging of the thoughts that manifested Jamaica's Road to Oman.

Chapter One: The Journey to Oman

The driver of the On-Time taxi cautiously toots his horn for the 5:30 a.m. pick-up on the morning of Sunday, January 21, but I had been up from 3 a.m. reviewing plans, unable to sleep. He looks a bit apprehensive … who can blame him ... "Coming!" I assured him.

Cognizant of our financial and managerial limitations, I had to be the forward team to Oman, to ensure that all arrangements were in place for the team's arrival and participation in their first FIH World Cup tournament. My wife, Rose, as she usually did, sleepily ran through the checklist (passport, cash, documents, toothbrush, medication from Dr. June Francis, and so on), and bid me good-bye for another travel engagement she assured me would be successful. No need to wake Diallo, my son, whom I spoke to about the trip earlier that night. I knew he would not be amused to be up that early. Despite an extensive travel history, this was the first time that I was traveling by road from Kingston to Montego Bay to the Sangster International Airport for a flight. Mine was scheduled to depart later that day, January 21, enroute to Muscat, Oman.

The taxi ride wasn't long at that early hour of the morning and in a few minutes, I was in New Kingston, ready to board the Knutsford Express, an excellent city-to-city ground transportation service, headed for Sangster International Airport. The driver of the Knutsford Express coach was professional and courteous. His strong, natural, and distinct patois-based pronunciation, overlaid with the attempt at standard American English created some interesting sounding announcements. Those announcements provided some amount of levity throughout the early morning journey for a few of the travellers while also reminding me of my many conversations with my colleagues at The University of the West Indies, Mona (UWI) on the importance of our local language and its role in our society.

It was while en route to Montego Bay, staring at the beautiful and lush Jamaican landscape peeping out from the morning dew and mist, and reflecting on the numerous developments along the journey, that I decided to write this book about the journey to Oman and the lessons learned along the way. All the hard-working people and teams affiliated with the Jamaica Hockey Federation (JHF) had pulled the proverbial rabbit out of a hat and created history. After 120 years of playing the sport in Jamaica, we had qualified for our first FIH World Cup tournament, especially in the new format of the game – Hockey5s. This bit of history should not go unnoticed; it should be documented in a book.

THE GLEANER SATURDAY OCTOBER 18, 1902 13

CIVIL SERVICE WIDOWS' & ORPHANS' FUNDS.

MEETING AT THE TOWN HALL.

MILITARY.

THE SMALL POX AT BARBADOS.

THE NELLIE LOUISE.

THE U.S. IN THE CARRIBEAN.

RELIEF WORK IN ST. VINCENT.

A NEW SPORT IN JAMAICA.

Hockey Match at Camp.

Following on a suggestion recently made in our columns, the officers at Camp and Port Royal have conceived an enthusiasm for hockey. They played their first match yesterday afternoon at Camp, and they propose to play another next week and to go in regularly for the game for several months in the year. A team from Camp was pitted against a team from the Port Royal Garrison, the two elevens being as follows:—

Camp:—Goal, George; backs, Jones and Grant; half-backs, Clutterbuck, White and Power; forwards, Lancaster, Ward, Tarver, Stokes, and Miller.

Port Royal:—Goal, May; backs, Wray and Scott; half-backs, Hearn, Shendling and Garnett; forwards, Lamb, Wonham Hall, Honey, Courtice.

The ground was damp from the showers that had fallen earlier in the afternoon, which was fortunate as tumbles were frequent. Many of the players knew nothing of hockey and others had only a nodding acquaintance with the game. Only a few members of the two elevens were experts, but they shepherded the rest with much vigour and soon got them to grasp the main rules and ideas of the game. A goalkeeper even committed the heinous crime of throwing out the ball with his hand, and fouls were frequent through ignorance of the rules. This was only to be expected. On the whole, the players entered very thoroughly into the spirit of the game and speedily became familiar with its technical points. The play was keen, but not very fast as compared with the average game in England or Ireland. One reason of this was that many of the players were obviously afraid of hitting their opponents on the ankle or the shin with their sticks—a sentiment which did credit to their humane feeling but did not conduce to fast play. The man who wishes to shine at hockey must be somewhat callous to other people's danger as well as to his own.

In the first half the game was fairly even and neither side scored. Soon after half time, Port Royal pressed hard and put on a couple of goals in rapid succession, Lamb being responsible for one and Hall for the other. During the remainder of the half, Port Royal did most of the pressing but no other point was scored. The best team certainly won, some of the Port Royal forwards playing a very good game. Passing was at a discount, especially on the Camp side, but that is a feature of the game which will doubtless improve rapidly with practice. After a few more contests, both teams will shape well and be able to offer a hard tussle to any other hockey clubs which may be started locally.

COLONIAL BANK'S REPORT.

A HOPEFUL VIEW.

REVENUE DEPARTMENT.

FOOTBALL.

SHIPPING NEWS.

ASHPHALT COMMISSION.

MURDERED IN NIGERIA.

Figure 1: Gleaner Article about the introduction of Hockey to Jamaica in 1902. (Source: The Gleaner Archive)

Despite my apprehension and thoughts about all that still needed to be done, for example, addressing budgetary shortfalls and finalizing our financial commitment for items such as airline tickets with Sterling Travel, the team was now set to participate in the first FIH World Cup tournament in our history.

Key Contributors to the Journey to Oman

Foundation Contributors

Along the way, in the rising morning light, I thought of all the critical characters, especially foundation contributors and players, who were responsible for my fortuitous leadership of the Federation and, for that matter, my involvement in the sport of field hockey.

Stratton 'Stratty' Palmer (That Coach)

My involvement originated from a direct but simple recruitment call at my alma mater, Kingston College High School (popularly known as 'KC'). Our Latin motto which guides my approach to life's journey is Fortis Cadere Cedere Non Potest, "The Brave May Fall but Never Yield". In 1983, my first coach and mentor, Mr. Stratton 'Stratty' Palmer, saw me walking in the schoolyard and shouted, "Hey, big boy ... What are you doing for the school?" "Nothing," I responded, a little cautious and confused. "Come and play some hockey," was his command, and from that moment began my journey, lifelong love for, and serious participation in the sport as a junior and senior national representative, coach, and administrator. Stratty played the role of the father of our hockey development. He was the coach of school and senior teams, guiding our technical and tactical development in the sport. However, and, more important, he aided with our psychology on and off the field, effectively guiding many field hockey players and immature young men (Hugh Thompson, Ewan Barnaby, Dave Lemard, Gregory Fender, Godfrey Christie, Rohan Fowler, Leon Kerr, and the Hinds brothers) to successful careers and lives as responsible adults. Many of the young men who passed through Stratty's coaching years have served as coaches, officials, and administrators to the JHF and other federations and sporting disciplines.

L-R Stratton 'Stratty' Palmer, Carol Cuffley, Fabian Stewart (Source: F Stewart)

It would be remiss of me to mention Stratty without mentioning Ms. Carol Cuffley, a former national player herself, who was like a KC's and KCOB (KC Old Boys) hockey team mom to our diverse and usually hungry young men. Carol's caring and understanding personality complemented Stratty's efforts at creating a family environment for KC's players, something that may not have existed in the lives of many young men on the team.

Donald 'Danny' James

The late Donald 'Danny' James, as my national coach, entrenched a philosophy for the many tactical training sessions that had us as players doubting the results of his many schemes. He would say, "Prove me wrong!" adopted from philosopher and Roman emperor, Marcus Aurelius.

---

2 Anthony S. Johnson, The Brave May Fall But Never Yield: History of Kingston College 1925–2006 (Kingston: Jamaica: ISKAMOL, 2008), 377

"If someone can prove me wrong and show me my mistake in any thought or action, I shall gladly change. I seek the truth, which never harmed anyone: the harm is to persist in one's own self-deception and ignorance." - Marcus Aurelius

I can still hear Danny now, as I have adopted the same expression for my philosophy of change or paradigm shift for the sport in Jamaica; as the leader, simply challenging my stakeholders to prove me wrong for adopting new concepts and changes that actually aided us on our pathway of development and ultimately taking us on the Road to Oman.

Donald James (1942–2021)
National, Club and College Field Hockey Coach - (Photo Lloyd Butler)

Jasmine Campbell

Jasmine Campbell, or just 'J,' was a national female player, coach, mentor and friend. She taught me what true love of the sport of field hockey really meant. Our many conversations in and out of season on the lyming bench at the hockey field, especially during the hot summer evenings, provided an opportunity for me to see and experience first-hand what unselfishly investing in young people really meant.

Her passion was evident in the guidance she unstintingly gave to the uncoordinated, impaired youngsters, to the talented and gifted junior and senior national players who all owed their playing careers to her. Her caring but direct nature extended to providing accommodation and help to many young, promising, female hockey athletes. Her loving husband, Mr. Campbell, 'Cappo', would simply remark that he was usually not asked but just informed of the new young residents.

I can't forget my time as a player when she cheered me on as well as chewed me out when she saw fit and provided me with my first real club coaching opportunity with the Tropics Hockey Club. While on many occasions we agreed to disagree, her life lessons of service above self and helping, particularly the youth players' progress in all facets of life, still resonate in her legacy of having people she directly influenced and assisted as part of the initial youth development program, now serving as coaches and in other roles. Her influence also aided in the development of my leadership philosophy.

It was absolutely great to see her son, Brian Campbell, in Oman. Brian is a pilot with Emirates Airlines, and he resides in Dubai. He drove 6 or 7 hours to catch up with Dr. Holt, who he regards as his godmother. As she joked that she knew him before he was a thought, I thought of all the many stories that are the reality of my functional and dysfunctional hockey family. So many stories of friendship and drama

Jasmine Campbell (1950–2017)

(L-R) Suzzette Ison Director of Sports, Fabian Stewart, President, JHF; the Honourable Olivia 'Babsy' Grange, Minister of Sport, and. Dr. Carlton Campbell, Director – Infrastructure, JHF; at the Pan Am Hockey5s Presentation (2023). (Source MCGE&S)

Christopher Samuda, Jamaica Olympic Association (JOA)

From early discussions in 2018–2020, President Samuda challenged, mentored and inspired me as President of the JHF, before I even thought of serving on the JOA Board, to think about extending my service in sports administration by offering my leadership skills and competence at the regional and international levels. He understood the importance of serving at a higher level and the mutual benefit that can be derived from offering my unique knowledge to regional and global organizations. In return for service, we could obtain a better understanding of regional and international structures, governance and finance and, ultimately, master knowledge of how to compete at that level.

Christopher Samuda, President of the Jamaica Olympic Association (JOA)

This was a charge that I took personally and followed by offering myself and being elected to the PAHF Board in January 2022 in Chile. Involvement at the regional level provided opportunities to create networks and learn how to properly bid and eventually host the inaugural Hockey5s World Cup Qualifier in Jamaica in 2023.

(L-R) Valerie Hall, Fabian Stewart, Victor Tomlinson and looking on is Nigel Harrison TRAVERSO participant, PAHF Congress USA/Pan Am Cup 2017 (JHF file Photo)

Our first quick pit stop in Drax Hall, a fast-developing oasis a few minutes outside of Ocho Rios … Time to get a sandwich and some coffee … crap … cold cuts… hmm … Oh well, at least the coffee is warm …. Rolling again ….

Elected to the PAHF Board at Congress, Chile/Pan Am Cup, Jan 2022 (Source PAHF)

Key Federation Contributors

Dr. Carlton Campbell

As we continued on our journey, I looked out on the beautiful countryside and the slight drizzle. I communicated with Dr. Carlton Campbell, the longest-serving Director in my tenure as President, a true friend, old college/club teammate, and genuine supporter of field hockey. This is despite my opinion of him being unfairly treated for his brutal honesty in revealing that he was experiencing tendonitis, which led to his non-selection for the national team for the Pan American Games in Cuba in 1991, where he would otherwise have been a sure pick. I told his mother, Ms. Daisy, it was her fault for raising him so honestly.

Despite the history, Carlton was instrumental in improving and readying our facility for all major and local tournaments, as well as building our first Hockey5s boards.

Dr. Carlton Campbell, CEO, CL Environmental Limited,
JHF Director, Infrastructure (Source: File Photo)

“Hey,” I said, while admiring the countryside, “I am going to write a book about this historic experience.” ‘Ms. Daisy’s only son’ (as we often called him) simply affirmed in his usual direct manner, “So you should, its history!”

Yvette Haughton

My next communication was with my former ‘work wife’, Ms. Yvette Haughton, a team member at the UWI Mona Campus; she is an individual member of the Federation and an excellent copywriter. “Yvette”, I said, “I am going to write a book about this journey and you are going to help me.” Without hesitation, she pledged her support, hence casting the die for these pages to be drafted.

Yvette effectively and quietly managed many of the communication and public relations efforts for the Federation, especially concerning fundraising, promotion and regulatory communiques. The significant but quiet assistance she offered to the Federation based on her skills and capabilities, was a great example of working behind the scenes. Without Yvette’s involvement in plugging the gaps in the JHF's communication networks and strategies, especially for the major tournament (the Pan Am World Cup Qualifier) and other events, freeing the hand of the President to address other critical management matters, the journey to Oman would have been seriously more difficult.

Yvette Haughton, JHF Member, and owner, Yvette J Writing (Source: File Photo)

Dr. Michelle Holt

My thoughts went to Dr. Michelle Holt as the ride continued through Jamaica's picturesque countryside. I smiled, recalling Steven Covey's words and our interaction up to this point:

"Always surround yourself with people who are even more talented and competent than you."

And for me, as leader of a federation, I ultimately must compete effectively for sustainability. I know that to win, you must surround yourself with people who know or understand how to win! Hence, working with Michelle, regardless of our strong and at times diametrically opposed personal philosophies and views on life and on the game, made for the development of an interesting but stronger team for the Road to Oman.

Our multiple, sometimes explosive, disagreements were only matched by our agape love for each other and our unquenched desire for the development of our sport and the accomplishments of the players and coaches. This unending thirst to first play the sport and win, then help improve the sport in general, bore witness to a woman who is a successful medical doctor, the only gold medal winning coach for Jamaican hockey (male or female) at the regional level (1990, CAC Games, Mexico City), who was now asked to return to national duties and continue to volunteer as my Coaching Champion, Technical Director, Sports Doctor and, most important, part-time Sports Psychologist.

Dr. Michelle Holt and Fabian Stewart in Oman, January 2024 (Source: File Photo)

Many people asked me and wondered aloud how Michelle could possibly perform all those roles, and somewhat feared her influence on various strategic decision-making matters and possible bias towards people in her own sphere. The answer is simple once there is an understanding and appreciation of the Contingency Theory of leadership (Fielder 1963). The situation or context warranted it!

Based on the unique state of sports in Jamaica, including serious funding and other human resource constraints (discussed further in Chapter 3), it is and was necessary to maximize the competencies of multitalented people in order to manage well. This is even more so when they have a desire to truly put service above self. So, we agreed that while I managed the complexities of the sporting bureaucracy (especially issues such as the perception of bias and detractors), as well as the financial constraints, Michelle would work operationally to plot the pathway to Oman with a very dim flashlight that we, the Board, provided to light the path.

Dr. Sharmella Roopchand-Martin

Dr. Roopchand-Martin and the tremendous work we did also crossed my mind enroute. Our meetings in 2017 provided the JHF with a greater understanding of the current scientific approach to elite physical preparation, especially water-based training and its research. Our mutual interests coincided – the JHF's need for a more scientific approach to preparing our national athletes (especially the juniors), allowing our coaches more time to concentrate on tactical preparation, and the UWI Mona Academy of Sport's interest in proof of concept through the gathering of performance data. The signed MOU governing the tremendous relationship, and results in our athletes' physical preparation and physiotherapy care, amongst other services, were pivotal in laying the foundation for the Road to Oman, particularly for the lead up to the qualifiers in 2023.

Ms. Audrey Gaynor

I remembered Ms. Audrey Gaynor, who served for approximately six years as Vice President of Women's Affairs but really covered both gender portfolios at times, based on Board defections and gaps. Audrey's unselfish sharing and caring for our youth players in developing the Saturday Youth Program was outstanding. This program was the genesis of Jamaica's first international exposure to Hockey5s at the Youth Olympic Qualifiers in Guadalajara, Mexico, in 2018. Four of the young men who were exposed at that tournament now formed the core of the national team to Oman (Christopher Reid, Nickoy Stephenson, Shemar Gordon, and Daniel Powell), while many others were currently playing on the senior national team.

Audrey Gaynor, former Board Member, VP for Women's Affairs, JHF
(JHF File Photo)

At this stage of the journey along the calm coastline, I spent the time intermittently charting strategies to address our financial shortfall and forecasting solutions for eventualities in our logistics arrangements as we journeyed to Oman. However, my mind kept returning to the many faces and situations that had just allowed us to create history. The collage below signifies the names and people that raced through my mind.

I reminisced on the support and guidance provided by a few of our regional and international partners such as Presidents, Albert 'Coco' Budeisky and Tayyab Ikram, PAHF and FIH respectively. And I reminded myself that I definitely needed to remember to get unique Jamaican gifts for President Tayyab and my friends at the FIH as tokens of appreciation for their support and assistance to Team Jamaica.

Michael Blair

I couldn't forget the contribution of Michael Blair. Michael is a sports administrator with extraordinary drive, passion and capability to execute sports activity. Rejoining the Board early in my tenure as President, for a second stint, he owned the Growth and Development portfolio with the focus on youth development. His organization skills and ability to motivate a team created a resurgence in youth development with a spectacular edition of the ISSA/JHF School League and U21 Junior League. His opening and closing ceremonies and organization of the leagues were professionally executed. However, his introduction and management of streaming the games and an exciting use of the JHF's social media platform, managed by a team of youth volunteers, took the presentation of the leagues to its highest local level.

Michael was also a major supporter of the paradigm shifts in managing the Federation and contributed tremendously to the strategies for the youth program and the Road to Oman.

Regional and International Contributors

Alberto 'Coco' Budeisky
President, PAHF

President Alberto 'Coco' Budeisky had continuously encouraged the JHF along its redevelopment journey. President 'Coco' created a direct line of communication with me in 2017 to allow me to understand the organization's operation, competition structure, and attempts at developing the game across the Pan Am region for all, including smaller nations. His mentorship and genuine concern for the development of the game, especially amongst youth teams, convinced me, along with advice from JOA President Samuda, to seek to serve on the PAHF Board of Directors in 2020. His advice, support, and confidence in the capability of the JHF facilitated Jamaica's bid for the Inaugural Pan Am Hockey5s tournament.

Over the years, our working relationship at the Board level has only served to deepen a professional friendship. Coco's advice, assistance with negotiations, and encouragement of our efforts to Oman was also well appreciated.

Photo of Alberto 'Coco' Budeisky

Tayyab Ikram
President, FIH

President Tayyab Ikram was also instrumental in assisting on our Road to Oman. An avid proponent of field hockey youth development, especially in his role as a member of the Olympic Solidarity Commission and the Association of National Olympic Committees, our paths crossed based on assistance to our Youth Development Program with information on Olympic Solidarity through PAHF. His direct style was well known; that is, calls at 3 a.m. based on our time difference with Asia, consistently providing information on key contacts, logistics and solutions to encourage and facilitate Jamaica's participation in the Hockey5s successful World Cup tournament.

While I have no doubt Tayyab's assistance was felt by almost all participants at the Hockey5s World Cup (especially smaller hockey nations), his accessibility as the president of an international organization (he answered or returns most calls) and passion for assisting small nations to close the playing gap with much larger nations and spread the development of the game was well known and certainly appreciated by the JHF.

The Sangster International Airport …. we are here … already! … The drive to Montego Bay seems shorter than I remembered but pleasant. Note to self … This experience wasn't bad at all… Why drive when you can be driven to MoBay? Hmmm … worth a thought …. but how would I get around in MoBay?

Maureen Craig-Rousseau (TTO)

Maureen Craig-Rousseau (TTO) (Source: FIH)

I fondly refer to Maureen Craig-Rousseau of the Trinidad and Tobago Hockey Federation (TTO) as my special mentor because of her wealth of knowledge (hockey and business) and the help she generously offered to me and the JHF, including the planning of the Inaugural Pan Am Hockey5s World Cup Qualifier in 2023 and the previous tournament in 2017. We served together on the PAHF Board where she held the position of Director and Vice President. She is also an elected member to the FIH Board until 2026.

TTO has had success at the international level. In fact, they were the highest ranked Caribbean nation in the FIH Country Ranking and participated in several international level tournaments as well as the FIH Indoor World Cup at the time of the Hockey5s tournament. Notwithstanding that fact, Maureen, a seasoned Sports Administrator from the Caribbean, fully understands the complexities of small island nations and the challenges faced. In our many conversations, she willingly shared her experience, solutions, and recommendations. Despite the friendly but intense rivalry between our countries (Jamaica, and Trinidad and Tobago), her ongoing coaching and advice on various challenges aided in the Road to Oman and continues to be valuable in our development efforts, especially at the youth level.

Sports Administration: "Damned if you do, damned if you don't!"

Having arrived at the airport and eventually checked in, I found myself at the Club MoBay VIP Lounge, continuing to work on closing gaps or loose ends for the traveling contingent to follow, while occasionally staring off into the distance and watching the arrival and departure of several airplanes.

As I sat in the lounge, I was also trying to reconcile an unexplained delay in the lower-than-anticipated critical funds from corporate Jamaica, the amount that was committed from the Ministry of Sport, the strange communication around the transfer of the committed funds, and the lifeline provided by JOA to avert the unimaginable.

I was a bit confused. We had an excellent relationship and partnership with the Minister of Sport and main portfolio agency, the Sports Development Foundation (SDF), which enabled us to first host the inaugural qualifiers, and now this! The challenges around Jamaica's appearance at our first FIH World Cup ...

We later learned that the publicity about possibly missing the World Cup may have frayed an otherwise excellent relationship with the Federation. However, I had yet to fully understand why, especially based on the critical and disastrous decisions facing the Federation as financial deadlines and critical payments for participation and travel on the Road to Oman loomed.

If only better ways could be found to have our major stakeholders in sports put in place policies and partnerships in government that will benefit the entire sporting fraternity equitably and transparently. While that matter may be material for more in-depth study and review, I remain optimistic as team sports in small island nations need the full support of all stakeholders to succeed or have any chance of development and competition with larger nations.

My multiplicity of WhatsApp conversations spanning last-minute finances, logistics, regulatory issues such as visas for Oman and Turkey, and last-minute well-wishes were interrupted by the announcement of the flight to Miami. With a sigh, I stood; it was now time for me to head to Miami, in-transit to Istanbul, Turkey, then Dubai (because of a delayed flight), and then on to Muscat, Oman.

Summary

This journey to Oman was historic. More than one hundred years since the introduction of field hockey in Jamaica by the British military, the country was on the verge of participating in its first FIH World Cup event. This feat could not have been accomplished without the myriads of people and agencies that lent their support to the development of the sport, its leaders, and the crop of players on this journey.

The journey was built on the grit and determination of a small group of active strategic and critical thinkers delivering service above self, as volunteers and contributors to the Federation and its diverse group of stakeholders. The inclusion of multitalented people with a high level of professionalism, moral fibre, and high hockey IQ was crucial to the development of the requisite programs on which the Road to Oman was achieved, especially the Youth Development Program.

The involvement of the respective national leaders – the Hon. Olivia 'Babsy' Grange, Minister of Sport, and President Christopher Samuda, JOA – was essential to the development of the critical path to Oman despite the challenges and issues involved in the final aspect of the journey.

The support, guidance, and assistance provided by our regional and international partners, Presidents Coco Budeisky and Tayyah Ikram, the PAHF and FIH respectively, to the development of our youth program and journey to Oman was outstanding and appreciated.

In the next chapter, we will be examining the start of the journey, the leadership of the JHF, and the development of a leadership philosophy. The chapter will also review the unique capability to utilize a multidimensional leadership style forged from life experiences that necessitated quick solutions to various serious challenges, to create the paradigm shift required for preparing for international competition. Staring Down Fear was a major part of orchestrating the foundation for the Road to Oman. This resulted in some key strategic activities and technical partnerships that were needed for the development of the Youth Development Program, the critical piece for starting on the journey to Oman.

Chapter Two: Starting the Journey

The journey of a thousand miles begins with a single step.
– Lao Tzu

A relatively short uneventful flight to Miami … Thank God as my knees were just starting to ache … We definitely need to consider the spaces available for bigger people on airplanes.

I strolled through Miami International Airport – not my favourite airport. Having been given mixed signals, I went to the wrong line, only to be turned around and marched in the opposite direction to get to the Turkish Airlines check-in counter. Note to self: inform my managers about this common but time-consuming and physically unpleasant mistake (and the long lines). My goodness, this is a long walk to Concourse E or F. Finally, I reached the counter. Dear Lord, that was far, but the counter wasn't open as yet, so I rested my weary legs on one of those benches.

My mind started to wander again, focussing on how Jamaica got to this point. Was it just luck or did our organization and strategic planning have something to do with it?

Well, according to Gary Player, "The harder I practice the luckier I get." So, I guess the Road to Oman may be a bit of both – some hard work and a little luck.

Leadership of the Jamaica Hockey Federation
The Connector and the Campaign Manager

I recalled that fateful visit to my home from Glen Patrick, a magnificent 'Connector', and Dinsdale Laing, a member involved with the development of the Jamaica Hockey Federation Constitution following the merger of the Men's and Women's associations in 1998. Their mission was to encourage and convince – or better yet instruct me – to offer myself for the leadership of the JHF rather than to serve as a director, which I had intended.

Glen Patrick and Dinsdale Laing seated on bottom bench, flanked by Dave Lemard left and Jerome Miles right. Seated above are Aubyn Ferguson and Thomas Herns. (Source: Paul Gascoigne, 2013)

Developing the Leadership Philosophy for the JHF

With Dinsdale and Glen as my campaign manager and chief organizer respectively, my initial reluctant agreement gave way and set in motion the plans for leadership of the Federation and a personal journey that challenged me to overcome some fears based on my understanding of leadership.

Leadership can be described as the process by which an individual or group of individuals influence others in an effort to inspire them, as well as other stakeholders, to move towards a particular end or desired goal that depends on aligned values and mutual benefit. Leadership and leaders focus on effectiveness and the goal of the organization, while management focuses on efficiency and process goals of the organization or individual (Pedersen & Thibault, 2018). It is important, especially in the volunteer environment, to understand the distinction, especially when forming a team and assigning portfolios and tasks.

The fears I had to overcome were based on lessons in leadership learned from two recent exhausting business start-ups in which I was involved that did not pass year three for several reasons. These had psychological and financial consequences, a subject for another book. The fears to which I refer, I discovered, are discussed in a book by Mark Divine, *Staring Down the Wolf: 7 Leadership Commitments that Forge Elite Teams* (2020). Divine's book, despite having a heavy military focus, is adaptable to real life, and adequately puts in perspective the fears I needed to overcome or stare down, in order to effectively lead our Federation:

1. Stare down the fear of Risk
2. Stare down the fear of Failure
3. Stare down the fear of Judgement
4. Stare down the fear of Discomfort
5. Stare down the fear of Obstacles
6. Stare down the fear of Sharing
7. Stare down the fear of Committing to a Bigger Mission

Understanding my fears and the need for change at the Federation also gave rise to a theme I used consistently for

Change Management (Chapter 3), the paradigm shift. At the Federation, unlike at my previous ventures, I would be in charge, the chief decision maker, and I would be held accountable for the organization's results. This position I now relished because I had occupied several leadership positions over my playing, university, project management, and professional life with some degree of success at doing things a little differently but fully oriented to achieving the desired goals. On the Road to Oman, it was now time to employ my capabilities to a difficult voluntary organization I termed my dysfunctional–functional JHF family.

Brief Organizational Analysis of the JHF in 2016

Some unenviable situations and facts greeted my presidency and Board in 2016. Despite the many positive achievements of the previous board members, including hosting the Club League, School Leagues and some training programs, as well as managing to have some cash reserves in the bank (despite the negative debt to cash ratio), the Federation was at a bit of a standstill.

Apart from the obvious governance and volunteerism challenges, the JHF seemed to have a leadership vacuum. Volunteers didn't want to serve based on their various fears, mostly of vicious criticism and internal conflicts. In addition, the need to manage the precarious financial position with a challenging debt burden also contributed to the situation the JHF was experiencing. Furthermore, the previous administration, correctly in my opinion, committed to host the 2017 Central American and Caribbean (CAC) Games but, unfortunately, without all the requisite governmental approvals and the absence of the appropriate budgetary considerations. There were many uncertainties as it related to overall goals and future plans.

It was also critical for our survival to resuscitate the youth program based on the obvious decline in the numbers participating in our sport, especially at the club level. Therefore, we had to act decisively and work on the priority areas while creating the required planning mechanism to create value for the other stakeholders within and outside the Federation.

Hmmm … cleared immigration and customs ... and yes ma'am, I'm in-transit to Turkey … I go here? Are you sure? Ok then, after 40 mins in this line … What Sir? … wrong line … I need to go all the way to concourse E or F …. Simply mumbling some quite Jamaican expressions … I need to tell the manager to avoid this!!

Understanding and Applying Theories of Leadership to the JHF

My understanding of theories of leadership and their application provided an advantage to successfully leading the JHF, as well as undertaking the change management that facilitated the activities on the Road to Oman. For this aspect, the use of the Contingency, Situation and Integrated Multi-Style Models helped to highlight how various approaches were utilized for administration and for ushering in a changed approach for effectiveness.

Contingency Theory (Fiedler 1963)

The Contingency Theory of leadership sees leadership as being based on an interaction of the leader and the followers in an organization. The interaction is influenced by what is termed the organizational complexity (how geographically widespread the organization is, for example) and the level of task uncertainty. Task uncertainty refers to the need for guidance for followers to execute assigned tasks.

Leadership in the Contingency model depends on:

- Power and goals of the leader
- Communication of the expectations and values
- Alignment of expectations and values

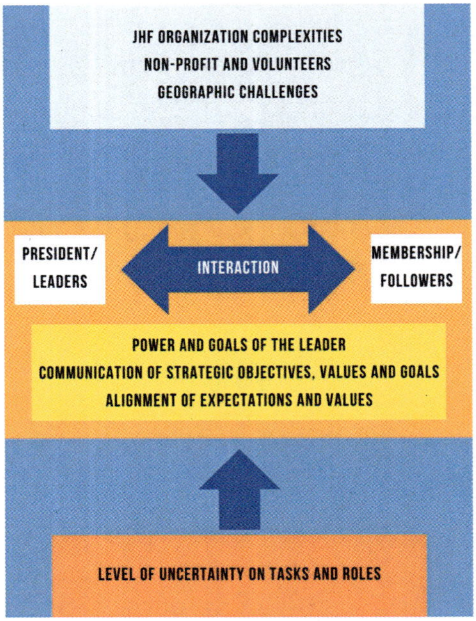

Figure 2: An Interactive Process: Applying the Contingency Theory of Leadership to the JHF - Adapted from: Pedersen, P. M., & Thibault, L. (2018)

Applying the Contingency Theory, to first regain the necessary trust between the leader and the followers, we had to use the power of the presidency and authority of the Board to align significantly diverse values among the members of the Board, Council, and ordinary members of the organization.

The most appropriate alignment in a specific direction came from an expedited strategic planning process. This allowed for the quick modification and explanation of actions and activities, while creating more certainty to updated roles and tasks. An example of this was the new Coaching Champion[3] and Document Management Expert roles introduced to the Federation at the Board level. The Document Manager was co-opted to the Board with the critical task of helping us to collate and efficiently manage our diverse data sets, with many different procedures and policies. This needed to be set up online for easy access by new committee and board members.

---

3 The Coaching Champion refers to a person that is responsible for the process to develop, mentor and advise the Board on coaching programs, especially for the introduction of the potentially new cadre of young coaches.

Situational Theory (Hersey and Blanchard 1970s)

The Situational leadership theory is an approach that suggests that you need to match the leadership style with the maturity level or preparedness levels of the followers. A preliminary assessment of our membership revealed a wide spectrum of competencies and capabilities amongst them. See the model in Figure 3, adapted from Situational Theory (Schermerhorn, 1997).

The following represented the maturity levels within the organization

M1: Low Commitment and Skills
M2: High Commitment and Low Competence
M3: Fair Competence but low Commitment
M4: High Competence and High Commitment

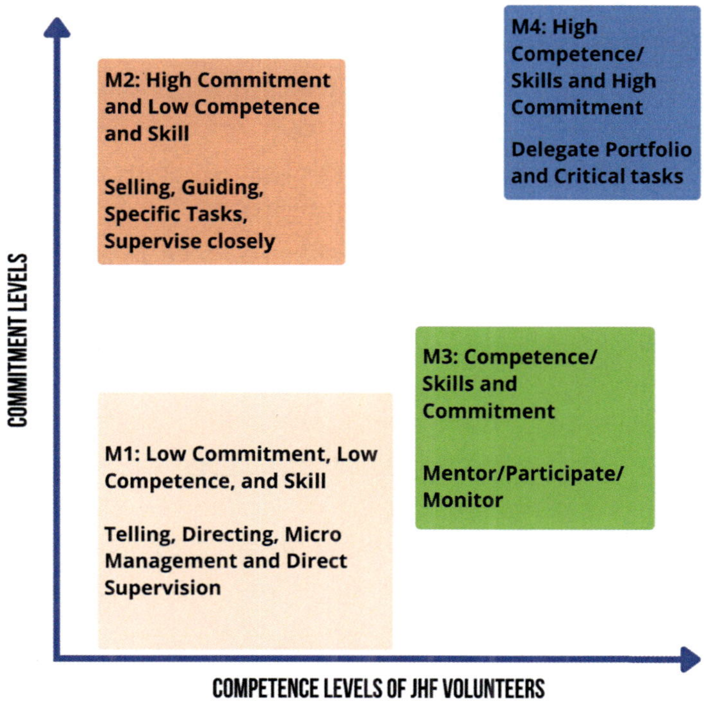

Figure 3: Adapting the Situational Theory to JHF (2016/18)

The situation that existed in the Federation, based on the assessment and model, indicated that while we required many M4 level individuals, the majority of the members of the Federation's management fell in the other categories, that is, M1, M2, and M3. This created a challenge for leadership, based on the number of qualified people required in a volunteer organization for the multiplicity of operational functions. This ranged from organizing major tournaments to technical operations, seminars, workshops, creating development and other technical reports for national and international engagements.

The fact that we had a large number of M1 followers meant a greater degree of specific and direct instructions had to be given to the followers on a consistent basis. For those who demonstrated the commitment but lacked the skills and competence, M2s, we provided a greater degree of supervision and guidance for various areas within the Federation's operation. The group in the M3 category also created significant challenges. The Federation had many competent people but, for a number of reasons, their commitment had diminished. Therefore, as the Leader, it was imperative for me to find a way to motivate, mentor and work closely with this group to increase their efficiency. This cadre had many young professionals who, possibly based on career changes or work demands, were not as committed as the workload required, but still had the competence to execute various tasks or roles when motivated to do so.

The M4 cadre was mentioned earlier. This group of individuals was saddled with a greater number of roles and responsibilities. Therefore, as leader, I was confident to delegate various programs, projects and portfolios to this smaller group of highly professional, committed and competent people. Thereafter, I would be assured of positive deliverables.

Cognizant of vast differences in the organization and challenging complexities, the new Board had to begin to organize and correct issues and challenges related to governance, finances, and the requisite competencies for leadership positions in the organization, in order to establish the basis to be effective.

Based on the preliminary application of the two behavioural theories to the Federation, it was clear that we had to engage a multidimensional or integrated multi-style leadership approach.

Integrated Leadership, a Conceptual Model

The Integrated Multi-Style Model, introduced by Andrew Hede in 2001, suggests that for effectiveness, there has to be a combination effort from the Leader Manager. This indicates that the leader has to be effective across approximately eight dimensions as depicted in Figure 4.

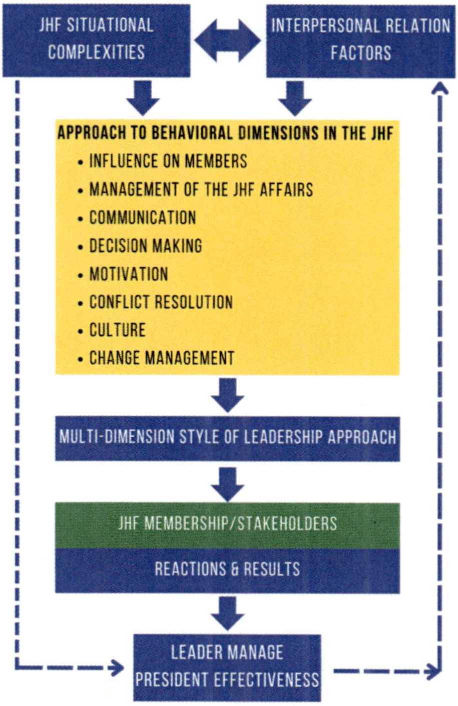

Figure 4: The Integrated Multi-Style Model of Leadership (Adapted from the Integrated Multi-Style Model of Leadership for Managing Behaviour in Organisations Hede, 2001)

As a result of the JHF's complex environment, with a few highly committed and competent individuals, a dynamic multidimensional leadership style had to be employed for effectiveness. In many instances, as outlined in the diagram, expedited decisions had to be executed in an autocratic manner for overall effectiveness. While working with some board members and committees, a more participative approach was used to allow highly competent volunteers to handle technical, infrastructure, and operational requirements with limited supervision or involvement.

Once various recurring tasks and activities were managed efficiently, the change management approach, the paradigm shift, required a transformational leadership approach. Once introduced, the concept had to be enforced and reinforced through functional activities such as governance and policy reintroduction or changes across the organization. The management of the communication was important and, at times, became our proverbial Achilles heel.

As outlined in Figure x, it was important to manage the change management process while keeping the membership motivated. Our Jamaican style of communication sometimes involves vociferous disagreements and may require dispute resolution strategies. Such situations required careful management but, also, involvement of the President and directors to address matters and guard against the perception of bias.

The Leader/Manager approach taken for effectiveness over my tenure as President allowed the organization to achieve various desired goals. However, the many uncompromising demands that I made when acting as Manager may have contributed to the departure of some volunteers who offered their service for leadership positions. The more task-driven approach of management (the President) seemed to negatively affect the commitment and performance of some volunteers in management, particularly younger volunteers. The approach may have reduced the recommended requirement for the President to be more of a motivator and mentor to those individuals as suggested under M3 of the Situational theory. This would have possibly sustained or increased their commitment. I will maintain that fewer, more competent and dedicated volunteers seemed to have produced more effective results. This approach may lack sustainability, however.

Leadership Methodology

An understanding of the significance and application of the theories of leadership assisted with the change in the decision-making approach, allowing our stakeholders to understand fully the statement by Albert Einstein:

"We cannot solve our problems with the same thinking we used to create them ..." - Albert Einstein

In the early months of my leadership, the Board set about modifying various decision-making structures for the Federation. This resulted in the formation and assignment of committee and portfolio responsibilities based on maturity/capability levels. Single individuals replaced committees that consistently failed to operate and deliver. For example, the Coaching and Development Committee was replaced by a Coaching Champion and an agreed Coaching Program managed at the Board level. As mentioned in Chapter 1, the engagement of Dr. Michelle Holt as Coaching Champion was a significant turning point.

The JHF's financial constraints and challenges were evident from an examination of our accounts. We were significantly in the red, a better way to say bankrupt, especially regarding meeting certain immediate obligations. So, we narrowed the focus to specific programs and aligned effective portfolio leaders with core competences to match critical challenges. For example, the President and Leader handled debt restructuring and cash flow management and international and regional relationships with a small group, while Dr. Campbell and his team handled the infrastructure, and Audrey Gaynor and her team handled other important hockey-specific matters, all cognizant of our resource constraints but, more importantly, the need for quick and decisive decisions.

Therefore, even in a short period, so-called problems simply became a matter for Board members to solve, with few panic or knee-jerk reactions. Also important was the transformational leadership approach, mentioned earlier, to build a sense of responsibility for solutions amongst volunteers. So, if a volunteer highlighted a problem or challenge, an anticipated solution was expected at all levels of management, reducing the focus from transferred to shared responsibility.

The Structured Approach to Decision-Making

In relation to leadership and decision making, I have consistently applied expeditious instinctive deductions or 'thin slicing,' a term coined by Malcolm Gladwell (one of my favourite authors), in his book *Blink*. This is explained further under the sub-heading "Blink: The Instinctive Decision-Making Approach". However, I will acknowledge the use of the Structured Approach to Decision-Making as proposed by Foster, O'Reilly and Davila (2020) in *Sports Business Management: Decision Making Around the Globe*, 2nd edition, where they outlined the structured approach as:

- Objectives that are well articulated and defined
- Timeframe/horizon period of decision that is realistic
- Alternatives aggressively pursued and examined
- Constraints understood
- Uncertainty explicitly recognized

There is also a widely used 7-step model used for effective decision making (Panpatte and Takale, 2019) as follows:

1. Identify the decision
2. Gather the information
3. Identify alternatives

4. Weigh the evidence
5. Choose amongst alternatives
6. Take action
7. and Review your decision

Sports administrators generally understand the above method and principles. However, as noted by Foster, O'Reilly and Davila (2020, 22), "Good decisions do not guarantee desired outcomes." This is due to the uncertainty within the world of sports, and its many uncontrollable factors, especially with volunteers and other unique aspects of sport and its management in Jamaica (a challenge which I delve into in Chapter 3).

One such example of the uncertainty of outcomes based on making good decisions at the JHF was the introduction of a highly qualified person for the position of Honorary Treasurer. This was a need owing to the many challenges and changes in financial accountability required by the Government of Jamaica, as well as the serious need for the development and maintenance of confidence in the organization's financial reputation amongst its internal and external stakeholders. However, the extensive recruitment and co-opting of feasible candidates were only matched by the impromptu departure of some of these individuals (four) after short stints. They each resigned from the position for various reasons, including new job offers, family commitments, and migration. The same could be said of the investment in various promising youth players who left the sport, especially after junior-level national representation.

Blink: The Instinctive Decision-Making Approach

Malcolm Gladwell in his book *Blink*, argues that many people, including coaches and managers, can utilize what is described as adaptive unconsciousness (often referred to as gut feelings) to diagnose a situation fast and correctly. This is based on their ability to recognize a situation. This, he explains, is due to the person seeing or having some cognitive recall in very few seconds of whether something is right or wrong.

He discusses the idea of 'thin slicing', a situation where, as he refers to it, the supercomputer in our unconsciousness quickly (in seconds) returns a conclusion that can be as consistently accurate (and in some instances more accurate) as the longer conscious situation (our usual structured approach to decision making). Using psychological research and analyses from reputable universities, he argues that some people can code the micro aspects of actions, activities, emotions or objects to deliver a very high and consistently accurate response or decision to a scenario.

I will submit that my background (a story for another book) may have allowed me to 'blink' as President of the Federation and see the possibilities others may not have seen, among them, our Road to Oman. First, I had served the Federation, my dysfunctional/functional family, for years in several capacities (junior, senior national player, coach (collegiate, club, and country)), and on various committees. Therefore, I had first-hand knowledge about the proverbial 'factory floor' that is the JHF.

For another quick reference, my life's journey thus far has been filled with overcoming various difficulties. In fact, I would say that making quick decisions to overcome obstacles in countries like Jamaica is a way of life. These decisions ranged from early tragedy and childhood trauma to a true understanding of financial constraints, and how to work through them. My life's journey also includes possible dyslexia, and the abuse endured because of what I now understand would be classified as Attention Deficit Hyperactivity Disorder (ADHD) in an era in Jamaican schools when this was not diagnosed or recognized, as well as having a son who is on the autism spectrum. Added to all this was the handling of discriminatory behaviours on all levels (local and international), taking risks, succeeding and failing (what I call 'lessons') in several business ventures.

The above experiences and lessons are often coupled with the trait of being a direct communicator and a straight talker. For me, what you see is what you get, and usually I say what I mean and mean what I say. This seems to be a trait that is not appreciated by people who have a strange relationship with the truth and, unfortunately, there are a few more people who fit this description than is desirable.

So, over the years where others may see difficulties in life, I learned to use the 'blink' approach and, by thin slicing, to expeditiously (possibly unconsciously running through decision-making steps) develop solutions. This was done so that I could consistently overcome hurdles in order to keep moving forward.

Therefore, I worked on creating a leadership philosophy based on 'failing forward' and treating every perceived failure as a lesson that I know is recorded for future in the expeditious decision-making approach.

Leadership by Failing Forward: 'No Fear of Failure'

It was important to build a culture at the JHF or develop an early understanding that there was no fear of failure, and risk-taking would happen to ensure value-added for all. Therefore, our real situation and the lessons from the financial constraints should not result in the usual fear of moving forward. This should automatically trigger actions that quickly signal that we may need to reprioritize, engage in negotiations, cuts, and/or redesign of budgetary allocation but still focus on moving forward or failing forward. This was an approach undertaken many times over on the Road to Oman.

The quicker decision-making methodology required the consistent reinforcement of positives while we continued to move forward, hence the importance of the strategic plan (Chapter 3). This reduced the time wasted on smaller, less critical matters for overall effectiveness. It also allowed me (us) *to stare down the wolf of fear* as we progressed but, more important for the

Federation, it significantly reduced the fear of committing to a bigger mission, that is, international competition, paving the way for the Road to Oman by the interrelated strategic decisions and actions, such as the requisite technical partnerships and making youth development a priority.

Technical Partnership Development

Memorandum of Understanding (MOU) between The UWI Mona Academy of Sport and the JHF

Engaging the shift in paradigm, the Federation signed a Memorandum of Understanding (MOU) with The University of the West Indies, Mona, to introduce the advanced sport science services from its Mona Academy of Sport for the physical preparation of our junior and then senior national teams. Although we signed the official MOU in June 2018, we had initiated the athletic program in November 2017 in good faith. The first order of business was the preparation of the U18 Youth teams (M/F) from the Saturday Program for the Pan Am U18 Youth Olympic Qualifiers, slated for Mexico, March 12–17, 2018.

From left: Dean of the Faculty of Sport at UWI Mona, Dr Akshai Mansingh, and President of the Jamaica Hockey Federation, Fabian Stewart, signing collaborative agreement to benefit athletes, on June 25, 2018, at the UWI Mona Sports Medicine Clinic, Faculty of Medical Sciences Teaching and Research Complex in Kingston.

This reciprocal relationship provided data on conditioning, medical and exoskeleton information, as well as practical training for UWI students in the Sports Academy. It also provided the proof of concept for the Mona Academy of Sport of its capability to provide high-level service to sports federations and schools. On the JHF side, most important, it provided exposure to advanced water-based and plyometric-type training for the young athletes. Additionally, the physiotherapy and fitness monitoring offered by highly qualified students and staff was priceless.

What a long walk to the gate ... definitely need to let Panton and Ebony know about this type of error ... Tired ... need a little rest ... Miami International!

Under the MOU, Dr. Sharmella Roopchand-Martin, Coordinator of the Mona Academy of Sport at the time, led a program to first administer pre-evaluation medicals for all participating athletes in order for them to qualify to join the program. The percentage of early disqualifications, referrals for secondary screening and discussions with parents about their children based on the examinations, cemented my belief in the use of these early screening methods for ALL sporting engagement, especially at the youth level.

Wow ... this line to check in at Turkish Airlines is extremely long ... And people are queuing up and they haven't even opened the counters yet!

Members of the U18 National Junior Players at a physical training session at the Mona Academy of Sports Pool, UWI Mona.

Dr. Sharmella Roopchand-Martin supervising youth hockey players engaged in water-based training

JHF youth engaged in water-based training at the UWI Mona Pool

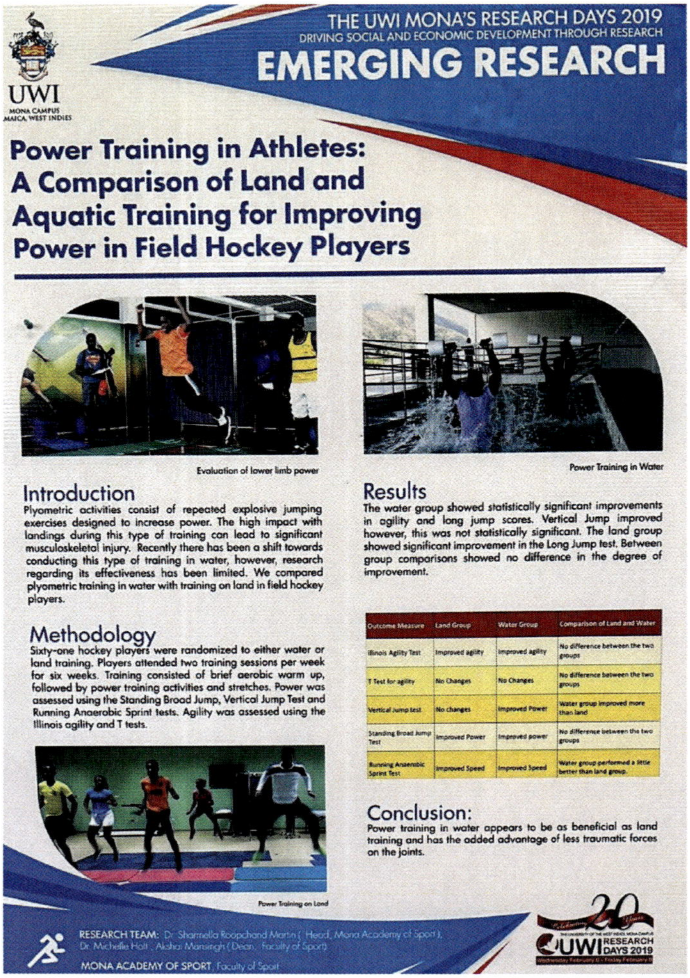

Poster showing emerging research (Bridging Gaps between Sports Theory and Practice)

What a line ... finally checked in and cleared security ... That took a while ... Why are so many people getting comfortable at this terminal? Holy crap! The flight has been delayed!

Pan American Hockey Federation (PAHF)

Under the Statutes of the Pan American Hockey Federation, Article 2, Commitment and Purpose, 2.2, by delegated authority from the FIH, the PAHF is responsible for:

> (a) Administering, encouraging, promoting and developing Hockey for both men and women within the Americas, at all levels, pursuant to a strategic plan that is developed and maintained in consultation with the FIH and is consistent with the FIH's own strategic plan, and in accordance with the scope and extent of the activity and responsibility delegated by the FIH

President of PAHF, Alberto 'Coco' Budeisky, as mentioned earlier, was certainly inspiring in his support of the program and Jamaica's efforts to redevelop hockey in the island. President Coco and I first interacted in 2017 at the PAHF Congress and later when he came to Jamaica for the CAC Games qualifiers. His genuine passion for assisting in any way that he could the development of the game provided stellar support from the organization for the Caribbean region and Jamaica, especially in the areas of coaching and technical development.

Jamaica's Youth Development Program especially owes a debt of gratitude to the hard-working Laura Macchiotti, Events Coordinator for PAHF and Coordinator of the Development Program across the Pan American region, particularly in Central America and the Caribbean. From my early introduction to Laura and our friendly quarrels, especially over her strict requirements for hosting the 2017 CAC Games qualifiers to the FIH and PAHF rules on our limited budget, we somehow developed a good and respectful working relationship. Over the years, she provided tremendous support and guidance for our involvement in designing development programs for the Caribbean region.

Laura worked hard to understand the region and its unique peculiarities and provided much support and information for the development of the PAHF and Caribbean region. On occasion, she would visit the island, in particular for critical meetings, usually related to hosting a tournament or seminars. She was always available for additional work, supporting the hockey program by meeting with the National Olympic Committee (NOC) and the Ministry of Sport as well as other government agencies responsible for sport.

The Youth Development Program 2017

When I assumed the presidency of the Federation, what we had was an ad hoc program for youth started by a few concerned coaches based on the many youngsters who wanted to play the game. So, Andrea Hoo and a few other volunteers would entertain these youngsters on a Saturday as best as they could. As many as 30 to 40 children from the school where she taught, Papine High School, and other schools such as Tivoli Gardens and Mona High School, would participate.

However, the structured Saturday Youth Program was started with an invitation to our schools for interested players to attend Saturday sessions to help develop their skills in the game and possibly be considered for the Youth Olympic Qualifiers in Mexico in 2017. Although we were in the middle of preparing for the CAC Qualifiers being held in November 2017, we knew the Youth Program had to be initiated. There was no doubt in my mind who was required to lead this program (Remember: surround yourself with people who know how to win.). So, I set about, shortly after I became President, inviting Dr. Michelle Holt to return and lead the program as the Coaching Champion/Technical Director. This was met with a bit of scepticism, reluctance, and a request for clarity regarding the direction of the program and her specific role. The simple answer: you are in charge of the program! Not a satisfactory answer to a highly analytical brain.

The process of my pursuit of Dr. Holt involved many quarrels about her interests, her previous experiences on JHF programs, and an inherent perception of bias that affected her credibility. Cognizant of previous conflicts, character assassination, and other challenges, I still appealed to her love of the sport, its young people, and passion for helping with their overall growth and development in life.

While I didn't get a clear-cut commitment early, the earlier adamant NO! was gradually replaced by suggestions of what must be in place to allow her to work and help our youth development program. Whew! A glimmer of hope in the summer of 2017 coming from what seemed to require divine intervention to change her mind ...

Since finding volunteers was a problem, as President and a former National Coach, I insisted on starting the youth program and made the comment and commitment that if I had to do it by myself it would be done, as failing our youth was not an option. At this time, Dr. Holt had not fully agreed on the program without a structured plan in place and opposed the type of start that I was proposing. But I 'blinked' and made the decision to start.

I recall like it was yesterday. Several children turned out in response to the invitation. That hot September or October morning, I stood there, alone, trying to work on this modern game with these enthusiastic children in the over 90-degree heat of the mid-morning sun. There were approximately 40+ boys and girls eager to learn the game and I placed them in groups so I could share my instructions more easily. I recognized I was being watched by Dr.

Holt and a young Devaughn Henlon, an aspiring coach at the time, along with a few other potential coaches and detractors. Dr. Holt had intimated that she was only coming to see what the hell I was going to do based on my insistence to initiate the program like the Nike slogan, Just Do It! without any formal, drafted structure for the program.

I suspect that after seeing my determination and commitment to lead from the front or, more likely, the fact that my over 300-pound, sweat-drenched body may have required her medical assistance in a short while, Dr. Holt and Henlon came closer and started slowly assisting from the sideline. I could hear their corrections from the middle of the field, sounding like music to the ear.

Then, at a much-needed water break, both Dr. Holt and Henlon approached the shaded area – I assume to hear my further instructions. So, it was the perfect time to announce Dr. Holt as the Junior Program Coordinator to the youngsters, and gladly and fully saddle her with the job of transforming our junior program and the next coaching cadre for the country. Thus began the steps toward the true coordination of the Junior Development Program on which the Road to Oman was built. Thank you, Michelle! The country and the Jamaica Hockey Federation and its family owe you a debt of gratitude.

The Hockey5s Boards

Amongst the significant changes that were being aggressively introduced was the boards for a true Hockey5s game. Hockey5s was introduced by the FIH in 2012 as a development game for youth players. It is similar to cricket's T20 format. Like the exciting T20 format of the game with a shorter duration (20 overs) and more attempts at making runs, Hockey5s has a smaller field, a faster pace, is physically demanding, and has multiple end-to-end scoring opportunities. The barriers that prevent the ball from

Ferguson (Boys) and Andrea Hoo (Girls), with Monique Lalor and Carol Hibbert as Managers (Male/Female respectively), and Yael Jagbir as the physiotherapist for both teams.

This team had the difficult task of pulling the program together for regional competition in approximately 4 to 5 months; that is, from November 2017 to February 2018. To increase the difficulty, the new Sports Science program from UWI needed to be incorporated in the preparation process. This scenario obviously created serious moments of tension and philosophical differences in the preparation of the athletes, and the seamless movement from physical training to field work with the coaches. After forming the coaching team, there was a bit of storming to norming and eventually performing. The major objective was accomplished, which was to have a young group of junior hockey players introduced early to high-level regional competition.

U18 Boys Team with coaching staff being presented to President Samuda at the JOA

The U18 Junior Boys team that played in the Youth Olympic Qualifiers in Mexico eventually had four members who went on to represent the country in the Hockey5s World Cup. Incidentally, all but two had not served the country as a senior national representative.

PAHF File Photos U18 Mexico

Christopher Reid

Shemar Gordon

Christopher Powell

Nickoy Stephenson

How did they perform?

Considering that they only had three to four months of serious training with 50% of that time extended to teaching those young students how to be serious student athletes, they performed well in Mexico. The Boys team finished sixth and the Girls, seventh. While the placements were not what was envisioned, the positives were immense:

1. The JHF had delivered on its commitment for an immediate youth program
2. We had exposed a young cadre of athletes to regional competition in hockey
3. We set the basis for strategically planned longer-term goals for the CAC Games and possibly international competition (the Road to Oman)

The Youth Development Program 2.0

Upon the return of the U18 team, and with the help of VP Audrey Gaynor, we finalized the construct of a Youth Development Program for the organization that further facilitated a coaching development program component known as the Elite Coaching Program. There was also an U21 Summer League organized in conjunction with the Youth Program that featured a very strong cadre of younger players who were participating in the U16 and U19 ISSA/JHF School League Competition for 2017/18.

The program was now organized to develop a strong team to meet JHF's intention to host the U21 Pan Am Qualifiers in 2019, for which the Hon. Minister of Sport would be the Patron (see photo of agreement, Chapter 1, page 10).

Importance of Volunteerism for the Youth Program

One of the most important and underrated aspects of the journey to Oman was the high degree of unselfishness and volunteerism provided by a few members of the Federation throughout the early program, as well as to date. People like Audrey Gaynor, Andrea Stephenson, Rudolfo Johnston, Michelle Thompson, Andrea Hoo Thomas, Aubyn Ferguson, Shenice Campbell, Carol Hibbert, and many others, contributed to the well-being and development of the youth players.

Their belief in nurturing and supporting the young athletes in this transformative process was inspiring, especially working along with concerned parents to ensure the maintenance of the students' academic performance while being in the program. The time spent, and personal income expended to assist with food, equipment, transportation, additional educational support, and other requirements, was truly remarkable and needs to be saluted. The effect of the assistance is still seen today, with many of these young people matriculating to job opportunities within businesses of our extended but still functional–dysfunctional hockey family and their contacts. They have also completed or are completing tertiary education, locally and overseas. The entire process along the journey transformed lives, a major tenet of the JHF's mission statement.

Hmm … I slept a bit in this terminal … interesting ... They are setting up a table with sandwiches and drinks! This seems like we aren't going anywhere for a while …

Summary

The Road to Oman was started by the leadership journey for the JHF made possible by Dinsdale Laing, the Campaign Manager, and Glen Patrick, the Connector. Influenced by their belief in my ability to lead the organization, I had to develop a leadership philosophy and overcome fears, including my own.

It was necessary to pull on my understanding and adoption of the contingency and situational leadership management applications to address the immediate matters affecting the organization and its desired goals. A multidimensional leadership style was introduced. However, while understanding the structured approach to decision making in sports administration, as President, I had to utilize an instinctive approach similar to that described in Gladwell's Blink to make many expeditious decisions to create solutions for the challenges and foster a culture that limited fear by understanding the philosophy of failing forward.

This type of fearless philosophy and leadership approach fostered the engagement of the Technical Director and jump-started the training program for the Youth Development Program (*Just Do it!* Like the Nike Slogan). It also allowed the Board to demonstrate the seriousness and commitment to youth development by designing and building the first set of Hockey5S boards, pulling together a Coaches and Management team, and financing their participation in the Youth Olympic Qualifiers in Guadalajara, Mexico, as the basis for the Road to Oman. All this done in a very short time period – five months.

The approach also allowed the JHF's leadership to orchestrate the requisite negotiation for advanced support from key local and regional partnerships; that is, The UWI Mona Academy of Sport for a scientific and database approach to preparation, and the Pan American Hockey Federation development programs.

Chapter 3 will highlight the introduction of the leadership of the strategic planning process based on innovative aspects of sports management. It will also examine the effectiveness of strategic planning on the Road to Oman, the change in management thinking and key elements of the strategic objectives from the plan that fostered Jamaica's journey to Oman.

PART II:
Sports – A Unique Management Environment

PART II explores the importance of strategic management in the JHF and the effectiveness of leadership in the strategic management planning process in building the foundation for the journey to Oman.

We will examine the planning process for the unique management environment of a sport volunteer organization and the introduction of change management thinking (the paradigm shift). The highlighting of aspects of the key strategic objectives or pillars, such as major tournaments and national team excellence, will explain the genesis of the Elite Coaching Program, the journey through the COVID-19 pandemic, the final suspension of the restrictions, and how the JHF facilitated participation in the regional competitions en route to qualification for the World Cup in Oman.

Chapter Three: Strategic Management and Leadership

The Genesis of the JHF Strategic Plan (2016)

It was abundantly clear that to make the sustained changes necessary to move the JHF forward to a higher regional ranking, and ultimately to compete at the international level, we had to have a modified strategic planning approach. This process I needed to lead. So, in the first few months after assuming the presidency, I tasked Ms. Patrice Clarke, VP of Women's Affairs at the JHF, to finalize a strategic planning document that she had previously started to develop.

The document was good but theoretical. There were gaps between the proposed activities and achieving the deliverables based on the reality that existed within the Federation. The document provided the basis for the new Board's understanding of referenced strategic plans from other advanced field hockey federations and their structured approach to development.

Leadership and Decision Making for the Strategic Planning Process

A Philosophical Foundation

The Most Honorable P.J. Patterson, former Prime Minister of Jamaica and a lawyer, in speaking to parliament on announcing a national holiday for Jamaica's qualification to its first FIFA World Cup in 1998, said in relation to

the holiday pronouncement being made without proper protocols having been followed, "The law is not a shackle to enslave; it is a tool of social engineering." My interpretation was that "We can't be shackled by our governance framework."

I am by no means suggesting anarchy or dismissing the observance of constitutions which are the fundamental guide and the cornerstone for the development of any sporting organization. However, in complex environments, circumstances change faster than any process for constitutional amendments to fully provide the requisite regulations in the modern sporting arena. There are several federations and organizations unable to appropriately regulate diversity and safeguard against serious matters such as harassment, sexual and otherwise[4]. Therefore, it is incumbent on leaders to review and make effective decisions for the good of their stakeholders, as best as possible.

The former Prime Minister's words teach an important lesson for taking necessary action and risks for the development and benefit of stakeholders for whom we lead. As leaders, we are ultimately responsible. However, the serious balancing act between creating value for all before the bureaucratic permission is satisfied, and requiring or asking for forgiveness later, should never be taken for granted or abused.

As such, the risk in effective decision making and strategic planning cannot be divorced from leadership. Leadership is extensively researched; essentially, it is your effectiveness while being at the helm of any organization, given the context and your ability to reach the aligned goals. This is an important part of the equation in sports management, especially for Jamaican federations because of the generally observed complexities and unique aspects of sports management, coupled with socioeconomic factors, as outlined further in this book.

---

4 For example, the IOC has attempted to combat these issues by introducing training geared at the protection of children while they are under the care of coaches and technical officials at training or tournaments. IOC Certificate: "Safeguarding Officer in Sport", https://www.sportsoracle.com/course/ioc-certificate-safeguarding-officer-in-sport/.

Changing the Sports Management Thinking at the JHF

"Decision-making in the Sports World often happens in a fishbowl with many from the outside making public judgment, often with very limited information, and with hidden or not so hidden agendas. Ever present in the Sports World is the very public backdrop of the second-guessing of decision makers, questioning of motives and criticizing them with the benefit of hindsight. This is an industry that is exciting to work in, but in which it is difficult to keep the incentives of key stakeholders well aligned ..."
- (Foster, O'Reilly, & Davila, 2020, Sports Business Management: Decision Making Around the Globe, 2nd ed., 4).

The quote above speaks to the type of decision-making environment encountered in trying to change the strategic thinking for the Federation, especially towards the Road to Oman. It should be noted that as an expressive people, our encounters, especially around sports, are often emotional, vociferous, and often counterproductive. In addition to the decision-making quandary outlined above by Foster, O'Reilly and Davila (2020), it was essential to understand the JHF and its membership structure to make the right decisions for our strategic plans.

The book *Managing Olympic Sport Organizations* (2007, 48) identifies the reasons why it is difficult to make changes in federations. These include:

1. *Differences*
    - *Volunteers or paid staff may not appreciate changes in roles, especially reporting channels*

2. *Competence*
    - *People may be uncertain about their ability to perform the new tasks required*

3. *The Ripple Effects*
   - *Change may have effects on personnel and channels unappreciated by people in the organization*

4. *Workload*
   - *People may resent the transfer of more responsibility or the increase in workload based on the change*

5. *Resentment*
   - *People may resent change as they may believe that they are not going to get the opportunities or benefits accrued to past staff or volunteers in the organization*

6. *Real Threat*
   - *People may lose their positions of authority based on the change*

While all the above reasons were experienced at the JHF, the main resistance was associated with differences, competences, workload, and the real threat. In the JHF, for example, the critical management changes that had to be made definitely meant increasing workload for some volunteers, particularly in the area of reporting. It also reduced the power base of many older and senior stakeholders, such as administrators, coaches and team managers, which led to a high level of resentment towards the leadership.

Situations such as this require a level of emotional intelligence and leadership based on the type of people for which you will have responsibility. John C. Maxwell, in his book *Leadershift: The 11 Essential Changes Every Leader Must Embrace* (2020), provides a typical breakdown of people whom you are leading. His 25-50-25 Principle, outlined in Chapter 5, "Pleasing People to Challenging People: The Relational Shift" (point 6) was fundamental to our strategic planning and activities moving forward.

Point 6 states that first, there are 25% of supporters that will like you and support your decisions wholeheartedly. Then there is 25% that will simply dislike you and any decision you make, even if it is in their best interest. This leaves 50% and they will swing both ways; that is support you one day and support the position of the 25% detractors another day based on where they are convinced of value. Therefore, it is very important, while not discounting the 25% of detractors, not to waste valuable man-hours in fights and controversy (no matter how tempting) as the 25% will more than likely not change their position about your decision or even about you.

While I had to learn this important lesson, once understood, I remembered an old African proverb that I used with detractors a few times working on the Road to Oman:

"A lion does not turn around to small barking dogs."

At times, the noise, distractions, second-guessing and criticisms grew loud in the JHF from various quarters on actions and activities involved in the change management thinking, the paradigm shift. However, as the leader, you must have 'vision' and believe in the process that you set in motion to accomplish the targeted goal. It is, however, very important that these aligned goals are executed and communicated from a properly designed strategic plan.

The Unique Management of Sports and the Strategic Planning Process

Sports management, especially in Jamaica, is unique and made more difficult because of the country's history of sport, which involves resources skewed towards the development of traditional sports such as cricket, football, track and field, and netball; the socioeconomic environment and demography. In addition to those macro factors, the following four unique aspects of sports management (adapted from Pedersen and Thibault, 2019, 803) increase the complexity within Jamaica:

Unique Aspects of Sports Management

- Marketing of Sports
  - Distinctive challenges in promoting sports

- Financial Structure
  - Financial base and its impact on sports management

- Sports Industry Career Path
  - Career development within the sports industry

- Power and Influence of Sports
  - The social impact of sports as an institution

Pedersen and Thibault (2019) explain the unique differences between sports and other traditional business management requirements. The differences between the management of sports and that of other traditional businesses lie in the perishable and somewhat intangible nature of the sports product – once the game is over, it is over. In addition, the customer's satisfaction is highly subjective, based on whether their team wins or loses; it is not necessarily about the game played. The financial base or structure includes highly paid players for some leagues and high capital expenses for infrastructure such as stadiums and maintenance but limited income streams, apart from sponsorship, with a high dependence on discretionary spending from customers to develop profitability. The engagement and influence of emotions as a social institution also requires understanding and skills for leadership and management. These features are usually not present in other traditional businesses.

A major challenge for federations in the Caribbean is the meagre financial base and its impact on sports management. This is especially so because most federations are not self-funded and depend on major sponsors such as governments, their respective NOCs, and the benevolence of corporate sponsors. Therefore, with high fixed costs for recurring operations, especially infrastructure such as maintenance of an artificial pitch, an office or offices, and supporting leagues, it is difficult to plan and develop without assurances of equitable and fixed income sources.

These unique aspects and features of sports management create a significant demand on leaders and managers to create effective plans. The planning has to be flexible to allow changes but rigid enough to withstand destabilization by any segment in the multiple layers of stakeholders. This becomes more important as issues associated with the financial structure become more difficult.

***Just out of a little slumber ... What's going on ...
a little scramble ... yup, the long-awaited boarding call ... Dear Lord, this is a lot of people ...
I am quietly praying that the seats can at least accommodate my small 6' 2" 300-ish frame for the 12- or 13-hour flight.***

The Effectiveness of Strategic Planning with Sports Management in Jamaica

A significant part of leadership in the Jamaican sports arena is understanding, according to Kane (2014, 4), how to "influence relationships aimed at moving organizations or groups towards an imagined future ... depending upon alignment of values and established mutual purpose ...". Therefore, it is essential to have people following you, that is, some or most of the 50% characterized by John C. Maxwell. One accomplishes this by having a solid plan where the stakeholders can see the value and purpose. This, I find, is generally made easier when the leader's assessment is based on Situational and Contingency management models.

Fabian Stewart, President, JHF, and Christopher Samuda, President, JOA. (Source: Loop News. July 7, 2022. JOA finances installation of lights at UWI-Usain Bolt Stadium. https://jamaica.loopnews.com/content/joa-finances-installation-lights-uwi-usain-bolt-stadium-614885)

Well, the seats aren't too bad … Got an aisle seat so my only concern now is my shoulder and knee with the flight attendants' carts … Tired as hell but need to send a few WhatsApp messages before departure …

In the very early days of my presidency, Christopher Samuda, President of the JOA, stated (and I still hear his imperious voice from our early days of discussions), "Fabian, every federation must have a plan; your federation must have a plan … what's your plan?" To which I responded, "We have but we are still working on it!" which was indeed a fact!

The fact was that based on the status of the Federation, that is, the Situation, when we took charge, we had to execute remedial tasks to remain functional. So, we operated on an internal strategic plan, prioritizing matters that had to be immediately addressed as discussed in Chapter 2.

As leader of the Federation, I felt we had done fairly well with stabilizing the critical areas of the organization during the 2017–2018 period, and with executing a few projects such as the Youth

Development Program. We now needed to convert the internal plans and thoughts into a significant but practical document to guide our progress forward.

In January 2019 for our planning retreat, the JHF Board (with new members joining in November 2018) and other stakeholders took the opportunity to have Ms. Novelette Harrison, Public Relations Officer at the JOA, as an external facilitator. The idea at that time was to build on our planning in a robust manner, having an expert from the NOC to guide our discussions.

She led an independent but serious and vociferous strategic planning session with the team. To say there wasn't disagreement on the way forward would be an understatement. However, as we grew to trust the process (analyse current, define future, set the goals and objectives, implement and evaluate) and follow where the analysis of the situation led us, the pathway and objectives became clearer and consensus emerged when we faced reality.

2020 Strategic Planning Session, JHF Board (Source: JHF File Pic)

Overview and Process

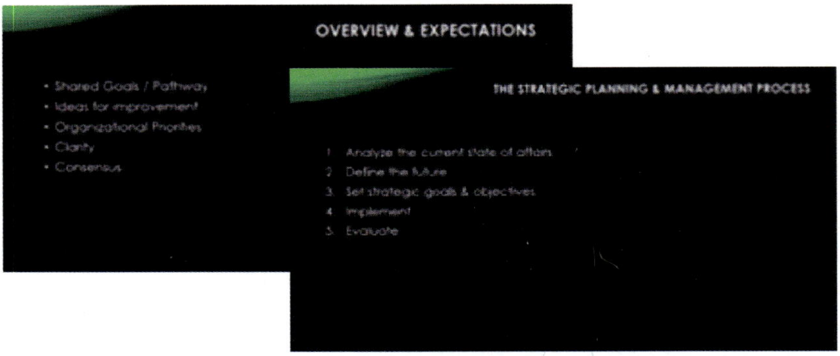

Figure 5: Extracts from the JHF Strategic Plan, Overview & Expectations, and the Strategic Planning & Management Process (Soruce: Jamaica Hockey Federation Strategic Plan, 2018)

Vision and Mission

"The only thing worse than being blind is having sight but no vision." – *Helen Keller*

We had to engage in a renewed visioning exercise. We needed to be clear on what we envisioned for the Federation. As Slack and Parent (2006) note, strategic planning "is the process involving external and internal environment analyses and visioning (vision, mission, core purpose) … leading to the establishment of goals/ objectives, specific strategies and tactics, benchmarks and indicators". There is that word vision again (visioning)!

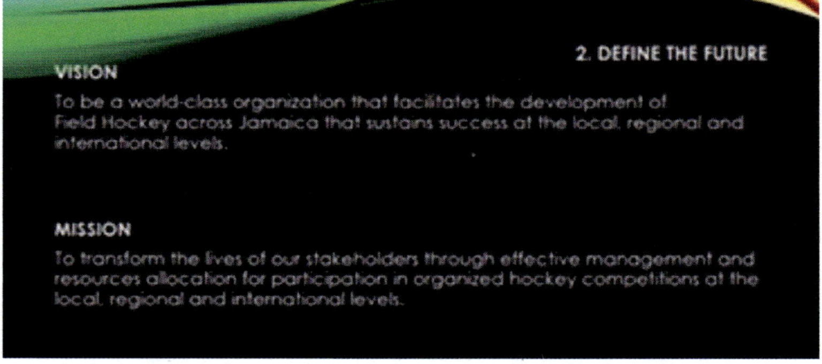

Figure 6: Extracts from the JHF Strategic Plan, Vision and Mission (Source: Jamaica Hockey Federation Strategic Plan, 2018)

Current Status and Affairs: An Analysis

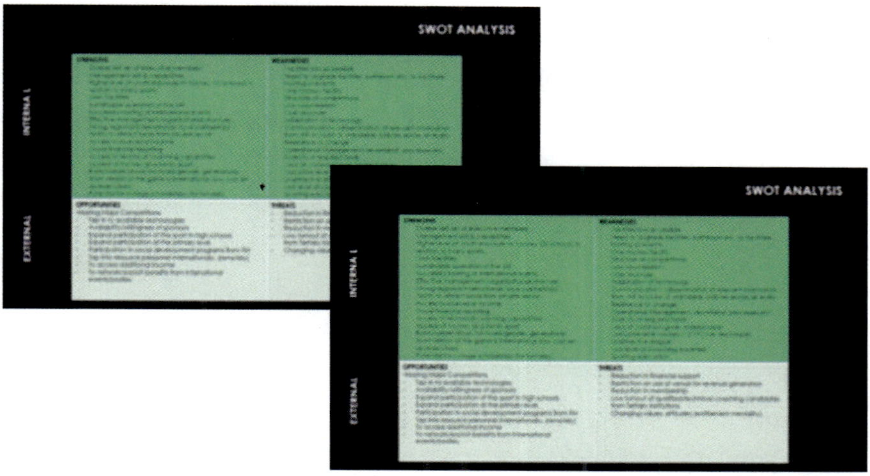

Figure 7: Extracts from the JHF Strategic Plan, PEST and SWOT Analysis (Source: Jamaica Hockey Federation Strategic Plan, 2018)

The examples above provide a snapshot of the types of analyses (PEST and SWOT) that were documented in the JHF's strategic planning process. As mentioned, the JHF may not be unique in its acknowledgement of some of the challenges that would need to be reviewed for the execution of the models (PEST and SWOT) associated with analysing the current environment. For example, the author's discussions with many federations and organizations reveal that most are concerned about the following:

1. Resource challenges (some are financially strapped for operational resources and equipment)
2. Limited number of qualified volunteers to operate in critical roles (human resource crisis)
3. Increased migration or loss of coaches, players and good administrators
4. More competition amongst federations or sporting disciplines for quality athletes
5. Approaches to preparation of Gens Z and Alpha (demanding much more for seemingly less return)
6. Communication challenges across the federation

These challenges appear to be universal based on my interactions with other federations within the National Olympic Association and across the Caribbean. In fact, I may be so bold as to add, from my interactions at the World Cup in Oman, it's possibly global, and especially evident for small island states and developing countries.

The Strategic Objectives

One of the most important determinations of our strategic process was to define, refine or modify the strategic goals and objectives. For the JHF, this was based on the five fundamental pillars on which we focussed:

Figure 8: Extracts from the JHF Strategic Plan, Strategic Goals and Objectives (Source: Jamaica Hockey Federation Strategic Plan, 2018)

- National Team Excellence
- National League and Tournament
- National Growth and Development
- Major Tournaments
- Financial Stability and Sustainability

These non-exclusive areas where various strategic goals are set allow for greater communication of the JHF's plans, as well as the evaluation of the activities associated with the plan. The symbiosis of the decision-making approach in the JHF's sports management, the paradigm shift, and the alignment of desired organizational goals, are due to repeating the strategic process on a biennial basis.

The leadership of this process and the continued updating and modifying of the plans based on the environment was instrumental in creating the JHF's Road to Oman, its first FIH World Cup event.

Knocked out of my slumber by the usual connection of the flight attendant's cart and my shoulder … "Ooh, sorry" in a soft voice, "my apology" … a statement I have come to hear very often on a flight … The things we endure for our country…

The Fundamental Strategic Objectives Paving the Road to Oman

... Woke up again thinking, Are we there yet? ... Slowly looking around at a sea of sleepers ... then quietly checking how long we have been in flight … crap … only 4 hours ... several more hours to go … Ahh … food time ... not sure how to view this … as early breakfast, lunch or dinner? … My body is confused but let's see what's on the menu …

From the strategic plans we recognized that the pillars (strategic objectives) were interdependent and that we were dealing with many different segments and stakeholders involved in the different aspects of sports. So, directors were assigned to champion in several areas that we thought needed to be prioritized. This was done in a matrix manner, allowing easy assistance from any director to a particular area based on their capabilities. This worked well because of the attrition that occurs in highly stressful voluntary positions.

National Team Excellence

As President, I assumed responsibility for National Team Excellence, because of the complex circumstances and the potential for perceived bias due to the strong representation from the St. Andrews Hockey Team, including Dr. Holt. Additionally, the sentimental and possible strong disagreement or discontent within this portfolio had the potential for friction in the Federation.

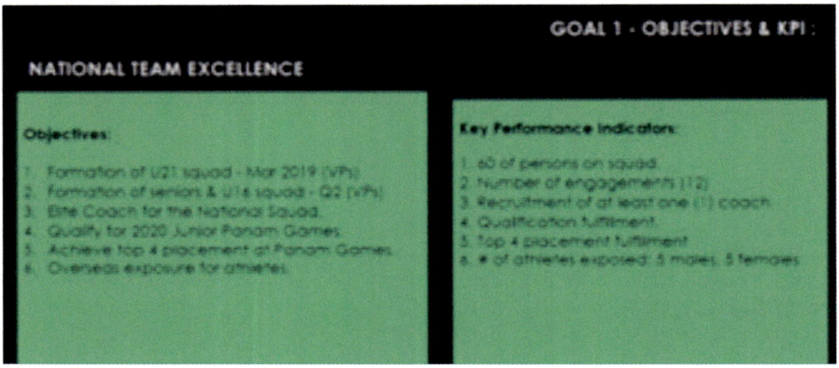

Figure 9: Extracts from the JHF Strategic Plan, Goal 1: Objectives & KPI - National Team Excellence (Source: Jamaica Hockey Federation Strategic Plan, 2018)

This area would normally, as per the Constitution and Bye Laws, be the purview of the Vice Presidents. However, attrition and the importance associated with the development of the portfolio, enabled me to justify assuming that role based on the indistinct authority granted to me by the JHF Constitution and Bye Laws.

Figure 10: Presentation of Updated Strategic Plan at 2020 JHF Strategic Management Session

In most organizations, it is implicit that the President, as the head of the executive body, has the responsibility to successfully operate the organization, in this case the Federation. This means, in areas of importance and value-added for all, I applied the fundamental principle enunciated by the former Prime Minister, the Most Hon. P.J. Patterson, and used our law as the tool for crafting the JHF's social engineering process – again, with due care to my power and authority as a leader.

National Growth and Development

The National Growth and Development pillar was eventually assigned to Michael Blair, a phenomenal sports administrator who usually says that he has never played field hockey in his life. But Michael owned the portfolio, firmly planting the seeds for the youth program, that is, School and U21 Leagues. His no-nonsense approach saw one of the best ISSA/JHF School Leagues and closing ceremonies in the recent history of our sport.

A section of the closing ceremony, ISSA/JHF School League

Michael and his team of volunteers

Up again. My doctor, June Francis, told me that I needed to get my big *** up and walk around on the flight because of my medical issues … wow … It seems I am not the only one pacing around and stretching on this flight.

To effect the growth of the sport and make it attractive to Millennials, Gens Z and Alpha, Michael, with a well-motivated team (how he does it, I will need to find out) introduced live streaming of the games and the resuscitation of youth hockey on social media. This was a first for the school league and definitely created a buzz for all stakeholders. Incidentally, I was traveling and proudly watched my ISSA/JHF School League Finals online at a Cigar Café in Miami. Cigar people are so friendly; my phone drew the attention of a few patrons because of my uncontained excitement while watching the games. Many had never seen field hockey before but watched with amazement the skills displayed by the young competitors.

I have reiterated that being conferred with the President's Award for Youth Development, which was collected at the PAHF Congress of 2019 in Lima Peru, was due to those who played a significant role in the development of the youth program.

However, the lion's share of the credit must be attributed to the innovativeness and dedicated work executed by Michael and his special team.

Fabian Stewart and Carlton Campbell Collecting the Youth Development Award in Peru

Based on changes made, the JHF saw both junior and senior teams competing overseas in the same year. This had not occurred for over 20 years. Despite this practice being attributed to the financial constraints of the Federation, the SWOT analysis identified the weaknesses and ill-effects of not treating the fundamental development of the next generation with equity.

The result of this challenge was evident in the deterioration in the results of the seniors in regional competition, lower competition for places on the teams, lower tenure or below par players due to the limitation of selection. It also further affected the production of good technical servants for the game, another serious challenge.

It was an understanding of the continued multiplier effect of not prioritizing youth in sports development why, with limited fear, we stubbornly and unapologetically set about prioritizing and crafting the Youth Program.

Major Tournaments and the Road to Oman

Infrastructure: Critical for the Road

The hosting of major tournaments was a must for the Jamaica Hockey Federation to increase the growth and viewership of the sport in the country. As part of this process, Dr. Carlton Campbell undertook the portfolio of Director of Infrastructure and Premises. The development of the infrastructure and its management was a significant catalyst upon which Jamaica was able to host international tournaments. However, before we were able to look at international tournaments, Dr. Campbell and his team continued slowly to refurbish the facilities for local leagues and tournaments. I can still hear our fights about the funds collected for the use of the field, that is, field rental, and its diversion to the National Team Excellence Programs, affecting his capital expenditure budget for further development and income generation.

Our journey to the PAHF Congress in 2019 was, among other things, to get a better understanding of the requirements, suppliers, and critical equipment needed for a tournament-ready hockey pitch and surrounding auxiliary facilities.

L -R Dr. Campbell and Fabian Stewart at PAHF Congress, Lima, Peru (2019 file photo)

Since we learnt some lessons from hosting the 2017 CAC Games Qualifier, it was important to increase our knowledge ahead of the intended hosting of the U21 and other tournaments, to assess the quality of our pitch.

Dr. Campbell's work in transforming and maintaining the facility since we came to office in 2016 is nothing short of incredible. He created and facilitated partnerships with contractors, engineers and architects such as Surdeen Construction, Christopher Bowen from Wentworth Construction and, eventually, for the upgrading of the building and offices, as well as the modification of the lights for night games. Carlton's negotiations and work with David Darling, Power Lighting and Telecom Ltd., for the procurement and installation of the LED lights at the field was nothing short of a miracle that aided immensely with the successful execution of the Hockey5s Qualifying Tournament. Lighting the Road to Oman in Chapter 5 will further discuss this significant achievement.

Again, understanding the value of people and their capabilities is important to the management of sporting organizations. Dr. Campbell's network and linkages as an astute entrepreneur and professional created great value for the organization. Additionally, his reasonable approach and somewhat calm demeanour (... but dear Lord, don't get Ms. Daisy's one son mad, though!) created tremendous business and regulatory credibility for the organization.

Having and respecting highly competent people in your sports organization is very important. So, having the likes of Dr. Holt, Dr. Campbell, Michael Blair, and Audrey Gaynor, to name a few, managing critical strategic areas of the Federation, allowed us to practically see deliverables and the important value-add returns to the organization from their sometimes interdependent and independent efforts.

Let me hasten to make it clear that other members of the executive team played major operational roles, such as Ricardo Panton and Dionne Smallhorne, the Rowe brothers (Lieutenant Colonel Ret. Roderick Rowe and Collington Rowe), and Victor Tomlinson. However, the earlier mentioned four have delivered significant service above self in their respective portfolios on which the Road to Oman was built.

The Bidding Process and Project Management

Another major reason for participation in hockey congresses was to better understand the competition cycle and be able to identify and participate in the bids for major tournaments that were in the strategic plan.

Hosting international events is a daunting proposition based on the manner in which sporting federations are financed in Jamaica, or should I say how we have to seek financing, as outlined under the section titled Unique Aspects of Sports Management, discussed earlier. Having and/or developing the capability for planning and hosting a major tournament and strategically offering your country as host in a bid, can play a major role in the competitiveness of the host team. This was evident in the home crowd support and overall performance of the national teams in the Pan Am–CAC Games and Hockey5s Qualifiers in Kingston in 2017 and 2023, respectively.

The interesting aspect of the bidding process for the inaugural Pan Am Hockey5s Qualifier was that it was a part of our strategic plan as a follow-up to the youth team going to Guadalajara, Mexico for the Youth Olympic Qualifier in 2018. Hockey5s is a smaller, newer, and more exciting version of the game and provides countries like Jamaica that place higher value on small entertaining games, to be more competitive in participating and/or hosting a tournament.

This is based on the reduced cost requirements of these tournaments versus the much more expensive 11-a-side tournament. Learning from the hosting of the CAC Qualifiers in 2017, the JHF had to work closely with the Government of

Jamaica to gather the relevant permissions to commit the island to supporting the tournament, financially and otherwise.

Tournaments are essentially projects and subjected to the classic Triple Constraint Triangle in project management; that is, the direct link or relationship between timelines, the cost and scope of work that ultimately affect the quality of the tournament (PMBOK 5).

Figure 11 : Project Management Triangle (Source: Project Management Institute)

Unfortunately, from our experience, we have had to be working in a flexible manner on several changes associated with the triangle. This is because regional tournaments, especially new ones like the Hockey5s or U18 Pan Am Boys and Girls, can have several unexpected changes and variations, for example the introduction or withdrawal of proposed participating teams. This will definitely affect the budget (cost), possible timelines on the completion of various critical activities, as well as the assignment of tasks and work.

Somewhat simple changes from the originally projected five teams per gender to nine or ten by PAHF, moved the Hockey5s budget from USD 130K to over USD 195K in one month of renewed confirmation. This prompted a series of meetings and logistics man-hours to accommodate the change in this variable. This also affected the requisite scheduling and timelines for meetings with the relevant government and non-government officials to finalize all submitted documents for final approval for the tournament, as well as requests for the required permits. The changes and delays also reduced the time available for the continued and adequate solicitation of support for resources, hence the additional meetings with ministry officials, and eventually the Minister of Sport.

Another aspect of bidding and hosting tournaments that will affect the Triple Constraint Triangle is the negotiations with the PAHF, the International Federation (IF) in our region. Once awarded, local federations such as the national associations (NA), the JHF, will be provided with specifications, usually accompanying the tournament contract, on the requirements for the tournament; that is, the roles and responsibilities of hosts (NA) and the (IF). These negotiations can be extensive (as Laura Marchiotte and Dr. Campbell can attest) as simple variations will affect cost, time, and scope of work that may ultimately affect the quality of the event. For example, late information on the increased number of participating teams automatically affects the number of officials. Therefore, if the NA, as hosts, are underwriting the costs of the officials, this automatically triggers renewed man hours and possible negotiations for additional auxiliary logistics and cash resources for the additional officials.

The typical project constraint demonstrated in Schwalbe (2017), provides a good diagram of the additional constraints involved in managing these sports projects.

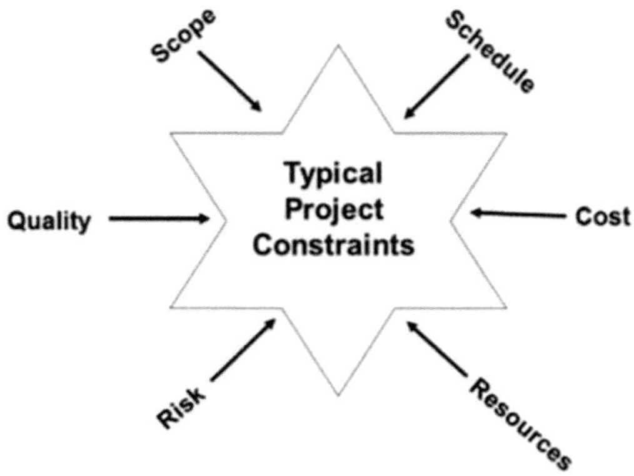

Figure 12 : Typical Project Constraints (Source: Schwalbe 2016)

While it is not my intention to take a deep dive into sports project management, it should be noted that larger competitions, such as games managed by the IFs (Pan Am Cup) or the International Olympic Committee (IOC) (Olympic Games) are well organized, financed and regulated. The projects are usually managed by and at, highly professional levels; however, they are still affected by challenges and issues over the project life cycle with many having significant cost overruns. Therefore, for NAs like the JHF, especially in what can be coined as nontraditional sports within the country, it is incumbent to understand the possible challenges (think Murphy's Law). Cognizant of these risks and challenges, sports administrators at the JHF had to establish and maintain very close relationships with all project group members responsible for carrying out critical tasks, especially in the activity planning and early execution phases of the project.

Jamaica's Road to Oman through the Pan Am Qualifiers can be used as a good example for a project management case study that featured strong leadership of an experienced project management team and the members of the Local Organizing Committee (LOC), including Dr. Campbell, Victor Tomlinson, Valerie Hall, Ricardo Panton, Dion Smallhorne, Andrea Hoo-Thomas, Richard Wisdom, Tanice Scott, and Shenice Campbell. The team was able to work through a tremendous number of critical tasks to adhere to all the established timelines by utilizing the analogy approach, basically building the Work Breakdown Structure (WBS) (PMBOK® Guide, 6th edition) from past successful projects, as well as the templates from the IF. The WBS is really the process of subdividing most of the project deliverables and project work into smaller and more manageable components.

Based on the understanding of the sequencing of tasks and the critical task, the Crashing method was used to execute the required deliverables. Crashing a project timeline is deliberately reducing a project's timelines by adding more resources, as well as possibly jointly executing critical, time-sensitive activities on the WBS. This allows for considerable changing of the timelines, including the critical path; that is, the longest pathway to deliver the project (PMBOK® Guide, 6th edition).

In order to have successfully crashed the projects for the Pan Am World Cup Qualifier, the team had to fully appreciate the various specifications for the FIH/PAHF standard of the international field hockey tournament. It was necessary to understand the processes of the respective stakeholders and manage the implementation of those processes in order to avoid disastrous consequences due to the effects on the project constraints. Recall the Triple Constraint Triangle – once the requisite crashing of the project was done, other areas must be affected.

The LOC of the JHF and the administrators of PAHF had what should not be considered as quarrels but vociferous discussions and negotiations. This was to finally arrive at compromises that would see the coverage of all critical areas which were the responsibility of the host, especially in the areas of infrastructure and transportation. Some allowances by the IF that admittingly affected the high quality of the tournament could be seen where temporary rather than permanent built structures were allowed. An example is the use of a large platformed tent as the second set of holding and changing rooms for players.

Through the crashing process, the team was also able to significantly and quickly identify the 'must do' Work Packages from the WBS. This allowed for the aggressive alignment of team members with a greater level of authority on a minimal budget to execute on requisite areas and quickly manage various challenges. This resulted in keeping to critical timelines irrespective of issues related to information delays, miscommunication, significant budgetary constraints, and many other changes that occurred over the project period, to ultimately deliver a somewhat successful project, that is, the tournament.

Through the crashing process, the team was also able to significantly and quickly identify the 'must do' Work Packages from the WBS. This allowed for the aggressive alignment of team members with a greater level of authority on a minimal budget to execute on requisite areas and quickly manage various challenges. This resulted in keeping to critical timelines irrespective of issues related to information delays, miscommunication, significant budgetary constraints, and many other changes that occurred over the project period, to ultimately deliver a somewhat successful project, that is, the tournament.

A Strategic Plan for the Road Is Simply a Plan

While I am very serious about the use of a strategic plan for any development and pathway, it is important to note that it is simply a plan. Unfortunately, the volatility of the inconsistent fundamentals in the Unique Aspects of Sports Management, and the manner in which resources are obtained and allocated in Jamaica, requires a serious degree of flexibility and understanding. For example, the JHF's national plans are developed and submitted on an annual basis for funding consideration to the Government of Jamaica and the Sports Development Foundation (SDF), the main agency for sports funding. This, unfortunately, seems to be a mere exercise required for the bureaucracy, and really does not fully support various projects and their scope in the strategic plan. Therefore, some of these critical projects for the development and competitiveness of federations (NA) are subject to the immediate challenge of being defunded (despite a promise of funding), postponed, or cancelled.

The next major source of funding is private sector sponsorship. This is extremely competitive and, at times, is closely linked to individual connections within the company (especially those playing the sport). Additionally, corporations and businesses may have different budgeting cycles and marketing and public relations considerations. Another challenge is the occurrence of major championships of other NA. In 2023, for example, the Reggae Girls (women's football team) and our Sunshine Girls (women's netball team), Jamaica Volleyball Team, and the lacrosse team all did well at the international level. This competition for funding from multiple NAs impacted the JHF's ability to attract sponsorship for the regional tournament. Further, based on responses to our inquiries, our subsequent struggle for funding to facilitate the participation in the international tournament in Oman could be directly attributed to the depletion of the marketing budgets of corporate entities and businesses that were perennial sponsors of the JHF.

This leads us to the very important pillar in the strategic plan of Financial Stability and Sustainability, an area for which our Board requires a high level of capability in cash flow management, where saying 'No, we can't afford it!' seemed a constant.

Financial Stability and Sustainability

The dreaded budgeting process

I recall a JHF Council Meeting, that is, a meeting of the club executive and individual members of the Federation, where I mentioned a quick 'back of the hand' calculation required to properly operate a league as proposed by the members. This was in relation to decisions that were made in order to proceed with the National Team Excellence activities as priority, rather than significantly fund a local, no-sponsored league under the League and Tournaments pillar for the clubs at that time. There was a stir as various members were in disbelief and one member challenged the accuracy of my calculated budget. I got serious and defended my figures to what seemed a surprised group. At that moment, I realized an unfortunate deficit in the appreciation of finance amongst our membership, making this a major source of disagreement. This fact led to reiterating and consistently educating our members on the financial outlay for projects and its impact on practical decision making and priorities for the Federation. This included the activities that would facilitate the Road to Oman.

The IOC's Olympic Solidarity Program speaks to the importance of developing budgets aligned with the financial plans originating from the Federation's strategic plans. This meant preparing annual, project (tournaments), and capital budgets[5].

Olympic Solidarity further points to the importance of developing budgets that are aligned with the financial plans originating from the strategic plans. Fortunately for the JHF, we were in the habit of developing the required budgets. It is simply the variability in real income from the sources of income available to the Federation and the changes in inflation and exchange rates that can significantly affect the management of this process.

A serious effort was made in the area of Financial Stability and Sustainability. However, like what happens for many NAs, the "math doesn't really add up". In any given year of serious competition or a major tournament, our Federation may require USD 250,000-300,000 (approximate calculation based on budgets from the JHF for fiscal years with major tournaments held) for complete operation for the year. The JHF is assured of approximately 9% of that amount from the government for its recurring expenses. Depending on negotiations, the JHF may receive an additional 35% of the shortfall from the Government of Jamaica through the SDF and/or Ministry of Sport. The NA would then need to find the shortfall in cash and kind from sources including corporate sponsors, the NOC, and self-funding sponsorship (plays, parties, and other promotional activities). This situation significantly affects development initiatives and attending competitions.

---

5 "Budgeting." Managing Olympic Sport Organizations (2007), Section 4.3, 177–184. (This was used in the Advanced Sport Management Diploma, Olympic Solidarity Program).

I was once told by a friend, mentor and ex-boss, Leo Taddio, Chairman of New Era Homes 2000, that once you are leading an organization, ensure that you sign the cheques and know how to account for the money. This is a lesson that sounds simple enough but is significant. It has stuck with me for a long time and allowed the JHF administration under my leadership to have engaged an accounting institution for the first set of audited reviewed accounts from 2017–2022 and the provision of annual financials for the organization every year from 2016 to 2024.

Major Tournament Financing

The JHF team benefitted from the budgetary capability of people like Dr. Campbell, the Rowe brothers, Audrey Gaynor and me – seasoned professionals. I can still hear Dr. Campbell and Roderick Rowe preaching to our younger management cadre to "put the numbers down, put the numbers together, so we can properly see what the budget looks like!" This was especially in relation to different activity expenditure (WBS) for the hosting of the major tournaments and/or travel to participate in a major tournament.

The message got through to all in the Federation and the serious internal practice of focusing on budgeting allowed the JHF to be current and on point with our cash requirements. Our media appeals and meetings with stakeholders concerning assumptions, variables, activities, and working budgets, especially any negative flows or deficit position, was seen as credible. The preliminary work on the finances allowed us to be able to quickly review, pivot and manipulate or re-scope work activities for limited impact to the constraints triangle, especially regarding the quality of the PAHF requirements.

We are generally open about our finances and needs but unfortunately, this has sometimes been misinterpreted. For example, although I did not use the expression 'bitter pill', an article was published in the *Jamaica Observer* about our financial outlook for making it to Oman with those words in the headline.

jamaicaobserver

41 likes

jamaicaobserver Hosting the Pan American Confederation Hockey 5s World Cup Qualifiers is certainly an exciting and momentous development for Jamaica. However, Jamaica Hockey Federation (JHF) President Fabian Stewart says that for local fans to enjoy the competition, his federation must swallow a bitter pill.

The media house and the reporter apologized for the sensationalism. However, the estimates mentioned based on the budgeting process and our understanding of the cost associated with running the inaugural Pan Am Hockey5s Qualifiers tournaments was factual and allowed for easy communication with the public, sponsors, and government.

As mentioned in Chapter 2, once leadership is based on aligning the values of stakeholders to an organizational goal, direct conversations can be had concerning the organization's financial affairs and its effects on decision making in a consistent and transparent manner. Further, if, as John C. Maxwell recommends, you allow the majority 50% to understand the rationale for a decision tied to the resource capacity of the organization, they are more likely to align with the leader's position. This is because they now understand that they are involved in adding value to the organization and enabling it to obtain its stated strategic goals.

Evaluation and Budgetary Control

Strategy Implementation & Control

The budgetary process aligns the resources to the strategic activities, objectives, tasks, KPIs, and deliverables. However, as mentioned before, this is a plan and the characteristics of the Jamaican sporting landscape, combined with the unique aspects of sports management, ultimately means some requirement for change in the plan. Therefore, as we had done several times for major tournaments and the Road to Oman, there is the consistent requirement to evaluate and re-evaluate what has been done and the reality of the situation, especially along the path forward for the project.

With a good strategic plan and understanding of our capabilities in bidding and planning for major tournaments, it was time for the JHF to have the audacity to stare down the Fear of Committing to a Bigger Mission. This mission was the qualification for our first FIH World Cup appearance in our 120-year history, as well as hosting the first Pan Am World Cup Qualifier for Hockey5s for the 1st FIH World Cup event in Hockey5s in Oman.

The tickets for the Road to Oman would be expensive and require many hours of work and sequential tactical manoeuvres from the preparation of the tournament to its actual execution. However, staring down and eliminating the Fear of Obstacles and using our experience, we forged ahead with the planning.

I have napped, watched a couple of movies, worked through some solutions for the JHF, thought a lot about the journey … and still we are not there yet. But I suspect we must be getting closer. Wow … this flight is long … Well, let's stand up again.

Summary

Leadership and the realistic strategic planning process was essential for any desirable achievement for the historic Road to Oman. A sound philosophical leadership foundation and an understanding of governance was also very important to making critical changes to the manner in which the JHF was viewing sports management. This enabled more flexibility, faster decision making, and results.

The unique sports management environment requires a flexible yet realistic strategic plan. This should include the analysis of the internal and external environment, paying close attention to the various aspects to be addressed for the strategic plan to be effective. This is especially so with the financial constraints and varied stakeholders' interests within the sporting arena and the Federation. Therefore, understanding and applying a proper budgetary process was essential.

While time consuming and stressful, engaging in a recurrent process of strategic planning, including serious evaluation, adjustment and prioritization, was the key to our Road to Oman. Working towards all the pillars of our strategic plan led to our success:

- National Team Excellence
- National Leagues and Tournaments
- National Growth and Development
- Major Tournaments and the Bidding Process
- Financial Stability and Sustainability

The JHF was able to focus on the Youth Development Program, matched with the Elite Coaching Program. This lay the basis for major tournaments and our successful bid for the Pan Am Hockey5s Qualifiers.

Chapter Four: National Team Excellence and the Integrated Effects

In the previous chapter we reviewed in a systematic manner the development of the strategic objectives or pillars for the JHF. It should be noted that plans are just that – plans. Plans require serious matching of the budgetary allocation as we operate in an environment where resources are usually scarce to execute various activities and affect achievement of our key performance indicators (KPIs), and ultimately, tangible deliverables.

As a result of the complex environment and the necessity for changes, there must be some degree of flexibility with the strategic plans and, at times, the planning process. Now, based on our goals, we prioritized the National Team Excellence pillar based on the integrated effect of its KPIs on the other pillars. The integrated approach to the execution of the KPIs formed building blocks for Jamaica's participation in Oman while laying the foundation for the further development of the sport, if the process is institutionalized.

The Elite Coaching Program

The continued development and focus on our youth and the Elite Coaching Program in 2018/19 provides a glimpse into the foundation of the Road to Oman. However, the full plans were disrupted by the COVID-19 pandemic in 2020. 'Life happens!' and, as leaders, we had to be flexible enough to change parts of the plan based on the unavoidable shutdown. Naturally, we pivoted and continued the Elite Coaching Program through virtual means. We will look at this later in the chapter.

The Elite Coaching Program was featured under National Team Excellence (see Figure 9 showing Strategic Plan (2018/19) with Objectives and KPIs). Thus, beginning in 2017, the JHF stubbornly set about undertaking the paradigm shift and transforming our coaching cadre to include younger coaches to complement the aging ranks.

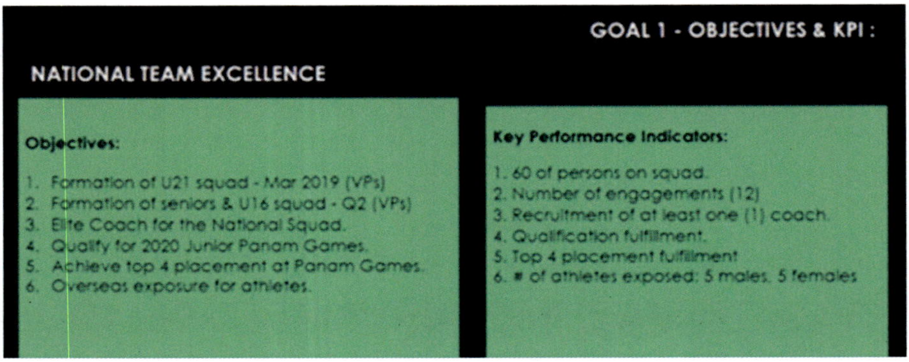

Figure 9: Extracts from the JHF Strategic Plan, Goal 1 - Objectives and KPIs: National Team Excellence (Source: Jamaica Hockey Federation Strategic Plan, 2018)

However, we should note that the program was also integrated with interrelated KPIs for the Growth and Development objectives. The need for the transformation of the game at the local level was evident. The requirement for the change in the way Jamaica approached the overall development of our sport became clearer to me while attending the 2017 PAHF Congress (held in Nook, Pennsylvania, USA) during the PAHF Pan Am Cup tournament.

The game had changed, and the multiple changes made the game itself more complex. Coaching and management of the game had been impacted by these changes. The game was now faster paced, required greater physical demands, and the integration of technology into coaching; for example, the use of GPS Tracking

Vest and game analysis technology (PlayerData, 2024) were now routine requirements.

I recall speaking to Valerie Hall, former international technical official and member of the PAHF Appointments Committee, on the topic of how dizzyingly fast the games were, especially with the consistent multiple unlimited substitutions. It was apparent that the days of one coach with one or two subservient assistant coaches trying to cover the critical facet of the new field hockey game and barking orders from the sidelines were over.

It was clear that our coaching setup that carried us into 2018 was extinct and, unfortunately, our results at the CAC Games in Colombia, after winning the CAC qualifiers in Jamaica in 2017, underscored the point once we entered a tournament against higher competition.

Recognizing the need for change, the Elite Coaching Program was born alongside the Youth Development Program. The aim was to assemble a cadre of 10 to 12 young coaches who would receive help to fast-track their development. This would include providing coaching and mentorship programs, assistance and incentives for completing external coaching certifications, and training. Examples were the Sporty Brain Coaching Course, based in the PAHF region, and FIH Academy 2024[6]. The Program was also involved with the younger players, especially with the advent of the U21 Summer League, to assist with their practical skills development. This gave the young coaches an opportunity to learn and practice specific coaching techniques such as half-time talks, game analysis, transferring instructions, and managing tactical changes. Additionally, it gave them an opportunity to work with a small team of coaches to introduce the coaching teams concept.

---

6 See FIH Coaching Academy, https://academy.fih.hockey/coach, and Sporty Brain course, https://www.sporty-brain.com/capacitacion.php?lang=en.

Introduction of International Coaches for National Team Excellence and Growth and Development

Kwane Browne, Ignacio 'Nacho' Bergner, Pablo Mendoza

To assist the development of the coaches and national teams, coaching visits were organized through the Pan American Sporting Organization (PASO) programs with PAHF. Kwan Browne (Trinidad & Tobago/United Kingdom), Nacho Bergner, and Pablo Mendoza, the latter two from Argentina, visited on coaching missions.

Both Kwan Browne and Nacho Bergner had itineraries that included youth development and coaching development. Kwan Browne visited October 22–27, 2017, while Nacho Bergner visited in 2018.

Kwan Browne (2017) – Youth Development Practice Session

Nacho Bergner at Denbigh High School (2018)

Development Program: Pablo Mendoza

Pablo Mendoza, a FIH Coaching Educator and Coach, was scheduled to visit Jamaica in February 2017 and after the full preparation of his itinerary and working very hard with Laura to make this happen, I was informed at midnight that he would not make the trip due to some unforeseen and inadequately explained circumstances. This meant cancellation of meetings arranged for the following day and loss of funds associated with preparing for his visit. We were not pleased, especially Shenice Campbell, the JHF's Administrator at the time, who had done the lion's share of preparing for his visit.

I have been told that I have a direct manner of speaking when angry, not hiding my annoyance, and using appropriate Jamaican language to express my displeasure. Therefore, you can imagine my 'warm' greeting when my good friend Kofi Hinds, Secretary General of Barbados Hockey and good Caribbean friend with excellent taste in cigars, by chance stepped into an elevator and introduced me to Pablo Mendoza while we were at the PAHF Conference in Peru in August 2019. Without missing a beat I said, "You are Pablo Mendoza, the … that had us in Jamaica set up for your … visit and you didn't travel … What the … do you take this thing for? What the … is that about?!" Well, Kofi, being a diplomat and a gentleman from the Caribbean, quickly suggested that we may be able to discuss the matter in a more civilized manner at the bar on the roof of the hotel. I agreed, eager to hear a worthwhile explanation on the missed visit. Pablo, who was acquainted with the Caribbean, having done a three-year coaching stint in Barbados, understood fully my displeasure and we had a full, open discussion on the issue at the roof bar and settled the matter over several Peruvian Pisco Sours. He made a commitment to visit the island and make amends in short order.

The Caribbean Posse at PAHF 2023 Congress Chile, L-R: Kofi Hinds, Cameron Burke (BRDO), Roger St. Rose (TTO), Nigel Traverso (USA) and Fabian Stewart (JAM)

Needless to say, in a few months, on November 6, 2019, Pablo was in Jamaica for a week-long training development and coaching workshops facilitated by Olympic Solidarity funding for the Caribbean and developed by the NOCs in conjunction with PAHF. This was a program for the Caribbean but Jamaica was the first and longest stop. During the week, he specifically worked with the U21 players and the coaches in the Elite Coaching Program.

Pablo's call on President Samuda and JHF General Secretary, Ryan Foster, at the JOA

The following is an extract from Pablo's 2019 report to PAHF and JHF:

> "Recommendations and thoughts:
> The JHF seems to be on the right path of having the sport, hockey education and overall development in a good and organized way, focused on a long-term plan. There is a good structure and line-up between Management-Coaches-Players.
>
> - Continue with the junior program development: there are a good number of players and potential to improve the level of hockey through these groups.
> - Continue to invest in youth coaches education, specially on the "Elite Coaching Group" which is in charge of the Junior Teams. They have done major improvement in the way of coaching throughout this period, focusing on coaching communication, speed and intensity."

The above validated the paradigm shift and strategic direction of the Federation and hence our way forward.

The coaching program was intense and well executed. Before he departed Jamaica, Pablo was reintroduced to the potency of Jamaican rum, a fact he had heard about from his father, Chiche Mendoza, who had visited Jamaica in the 1990s.

Are we there yet? … more food again … Is this breakfast, lunch or dinner? … Just not sure and my stomach is a little confused … But hey … let's see what's on the menu …

The COVID-19 Pandemic and the Road to Oman

"In the middle of difficulty lies opportunity." Albert Einstein

The quote from Albert Einstein sums up the leadership approach to the COVID-19 pandemic that significantly derailed the youth program. The program had seen a progressive increase in the participation of schools and young people in the sport, year over year from 2017.

The Ministry of Sport had ordered all Inter-Secondary Schools Association (ISSA) competitions to cease effective March 13, 2019, in the middle of the U19 ISSA/JHF School League. The closure would last until December 2022, a devastating and disastrous period for many sports, including field hockey. The ISSA/JHF tournament did not return until February 2023, further affecting the development of juniors.

However, in the midst of all the difficulties, the Elite Coaching Program and small groups continued to meet at convenient physical locations. But more importantly, Pablo continued his work with the Elite group by delivering online coaching sessions and seminars. He also allowed coaches to continue their development over the period of the lockdown.

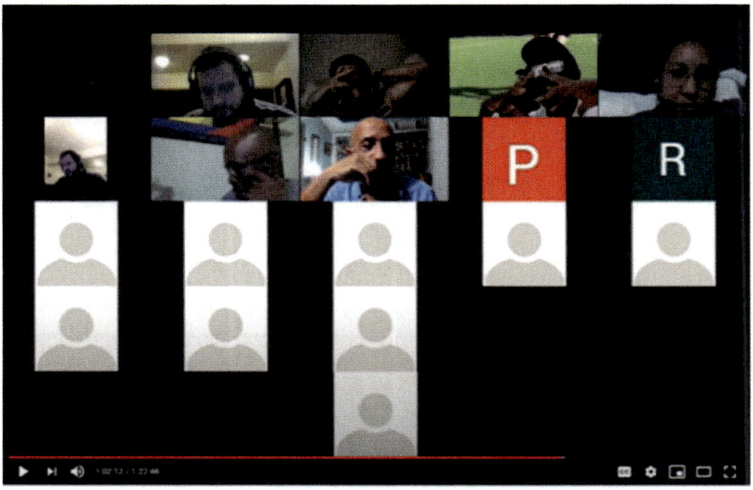

Screen shot of Pablo's virtual training sessions

These virtual solutions were facilitated by PAHF through funding from the IOC/NOCs to pay for Pablo's coaching hours and, at times, coaches from around the world were invited.

Coach Devaughn Henlon as #1

Coach Devaughn Henlon

Another aspect of Pablo's contribution to the Road to Oman was his identification of Devaughn Henlon as a prospective coach. Henlon, at the time, was in the process of making the move from being an international umpire to a coach. After Pablo's visit to the island and follow-up work with the cadre of coaches, both in and external to the Elite Coaching Program, we had a conversation concerning his recommendations and, to my surprise, he identified and praised Devaughn Henlon as one of the best coaching prospects in the program.

I am on record as indicating that Coach Henlon has an interesting personality that "simply only a mother could love". Brash, temperamental, bordering on rude at times but passionate about the game and his players. As I had seen over his tenure, especially from his first assignment in the CAC Qualifiers in Bermuda and other tournaments, he was above average tactically, a student of the game (not to mention his knowledge of the game from his stint as an international umpire), and he demonstrated the ability to be a successful conductor of a group of players that other coaches may hesitate to want to lead. Some of these qualities challenged working relationships but I trusted that with Dr. Holt's continued mentorship and that of others, he would listen and balance his good hockey IQ with the requisite people skills to improve and create growth and possibly become the most successful coach during his tenure at the head of the national program.

However, simply put, Pablo was correct in his assessment of Coach Henlon's ability and this was proven by the results of the ultimate qualification through the Hockey5s match between Jamaica and Paraguay. With Henlon coached by Pablo, and Jamaica coached by Henlon, Jamaica secured the bronze medal and a place on the Road to Oman.

Back on the Road: Lifting of the COVID-19 Restrictions

The government approval to reopen the JHF grounds for national training was granted only after our fourth amended submission (this after the addition of new forms, requests for additional information or new requirements after each submission).

Following an inspection of the Mona Hockey Field and the measures we had implemented, we received approval, dated December 30, 2021, to reopen for national training.

The continued work, virtual coaching and private sessions done with the small groups and the Elite coaching teams during the lockdown period facilitated a bold but dynamic opportunity. We managed to put together two squads and a functional coaching team, and then find funding of JMD 10M+, all in the space of three months, to participate in the CAC Games Qualifiers in Hamilton, Bermuda in April 2022. In other words, pulling the proverbial rabbit from the hat.

Our efforts again were aided by the JOA, SDF, Ministry of Sport, and several local sponsors. Mr. Seymour Barclay and members of the Jamaica Association (Bermuda) supported Team Jamaica.

This very vocal cheering party at our games significantly helped to eliminate any gaps in nutrition, transportation, motivation and other amenities for the teams while they were in Bermuda at the tournament.

Qualifying CAC Male team in Bermuda 2022

The decision and the work involved to get the teams to the qualifiers resulted in the Jamaican Men's team winning the competition and gaining automatic qualification to the CAC Games 2023, while our Women finished in third position. They, however, would go on to gain qualification to the CAC Tournament on a technicality. What was very important for the program was that it was a group of primarily young players, most earning their first senior national cap for Jamaica at the tournament, that achieved the tournament's success. It was also clear that an integrated group coaching methodology was now being employed successfully.

The Coaching Team Concept for the Road

The tournament cemented the development of a lower cost but effective approach to the ideal situation of a larger specialized coaching staff for a national team. Dr. Holt, Devaughn Henlon, and Nicole Bradshaw were at the helm of the program, along with the designated head coaches. Dana Sutherland, Kameisha 'Polly' Erskine, Tyrone Vernon, player-coach, and Yael Ragbir as the physiotherapist for both teams assisted them. However, what was observed was that all the coaches and managers were involved in some measure with the preparation and game time coaching of both the Men's and the Women's team. Assignments, recommendations, recording and/or analysis of the games were executed from various locations on the grounds. The coaching teams met for debriefings and seemed to be working quite well together. Additionally, we were now seeing the emergence of the young group of players from the investment in the Youth Development Program, along with increasing trust for their young coaches, male and female.

The success of participation in the CAC Qualifiers in Bermuda, the young coaching cadre, and a youthful player group increasing in confidence, set the tone for the Road to Oman.

Summary

The previous chapter highlighted the development of the Elite Coaching Program that was essential for the Road to Oman. Over the period, several international coaches visited the island as part of development programs, especially for youth. However, our introduction to Pablo Mendoza and the relationship that developed with the Elite coaches and the youth program provided the backdrop for the virtual work done during the COVID-19 lockdown period. The emergence of National Coach, Devaughn Henlon, and the basis of success post the COVID-19 period, especially utilizing the new coaching teams' concept, may be credited to both Technical Director, Dr. Holt, and Trainer/Elite Coach, Pablo Mendoza.

With the foundation set, it is only right that we now focus on the tremendous work that was undertaken leading up to the tournament. There were interesting challenges, solutions and people that effectively worked to execute the inaugural and memorable Pan American Hockey5s World Cup Qualifier in Kingston, Jamaica.

Part III:
A Rocky Road to Oman

Planning a major sporting event is not for the faint of heart. However, with the pillars in mind and our long-term objectives, there was no other option for the JHF but to step up and execute.

As such, Chapters 5 to 8 look at the finer aspects of event management in sports, the planning and implementation process for the Pan American Hockey5s World Cup Qualifying tournament in Jamaica, and its execution (The Tournament).

This was a major milestone as we were the first country to host a qualification tournament for the Hockey5s World Cup in the Pan Am region. But it was also a rocky road to Oman after the team's qualification and an enlightening experience in Oman at the championship that led to many lessons learned – all of which we explore throughout the rest of this book.

Figure 13 : The PAHF Hockey5s Olympic Qualifier Logo (Source: PAHF, 2023)

Chapter Five: Prepping for the World Cup Qualifiers

Preparation Work for the Tournament

Marva Bernard

Some years ago, I had a conversation with Marva Bernard, former Jamaica Netball Association and Americas Federation of Netball Associations (AFNA) President. She told me in her own demonstrative manner how, as President of Netball, once you are the organizer of a tournament, you are less likely to watch one full match in the competition comfortably based on the workload and consistent challenges. Marva, I can now attest to that fact based on the Pan American World Cup Hockey5s Qualifier, held in Kingston, Jamaica, June 4–11, 2023. You were correct! But you forgot to warn me about the preparation workload ...

In furtherance of the objectives outlined in our Strategic Plan, in the Call for Bids in 2020/1, the JHF submitted a bid for and were awarded the hosting of the inaugural PAHF World Cup Hockey5s Qualifier for 2023. We were comfortable with our efforts with the U18 Youth Olympic teams and our perceived vision of Hockey5s as fitting our capabilities through the number of quality players and the cost structure the smaller game presented. This made the decision to bid much easier to sell to the Board and Federation.

In addition, we also understood our capabilities to host an event from hosting the 2017 CAC Games Qualifier, as well as the benefits to the development of the game locally and possibly the infrastructure legacy for the Federation, these being standard benefits from hosting tournaments. However, we had a significant challenge.

The exhausting attempt to participate in the CAC Qualifiers in April 2022, and the pressing work on a recovery plan to have hockey played post the COVID-19 pandemic, led to some degree of uncertainty amongst clubs as to their ability to have a normal return to playing the game and be ready to host a tournament.

We nonetheless started to put the pieces in place for the tournament by ensuring the submission of the application to the Government of Jamaica, through the Ministry of Sport, and the discussions on the rationale for the tournament. With the approval being granted, the coaching teams were contracted, and we named a Local Organizing Committee (LOC) that was to be chaired by Leon Mitchell, a former JHF President.

PAHF Event Management Workshop

Coincidentally, the PAHF Board had agreed to host an Event Management Workshop in Jamaica in January 2023. The facilitators were Laura Macchiotti, PAHF Event Coordinator, and Maureen Craig-Rousseau, long-standing PAHF and FIH Board Member and a mentor. This successful event saw the participation of some 20 people face-to-face, and approximately 40 who joined online from around the Caribbean region.

The timing of the workshop facilitated important discussions between Laura and Maureen with the LOC to review Jamaica's preparedness for the Pan Am Qualifiers and provide assistance with the gaps in our planning.

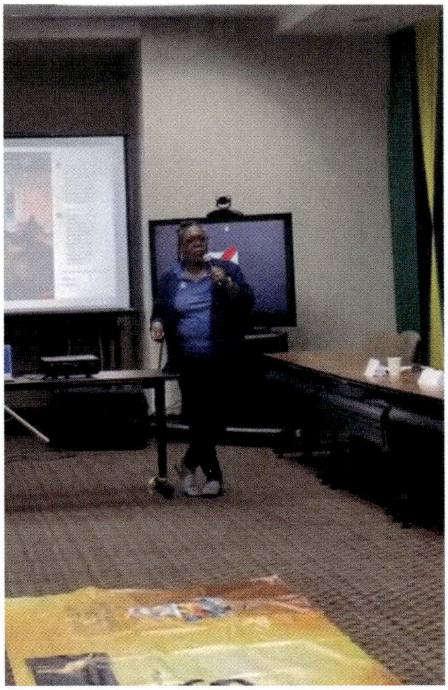

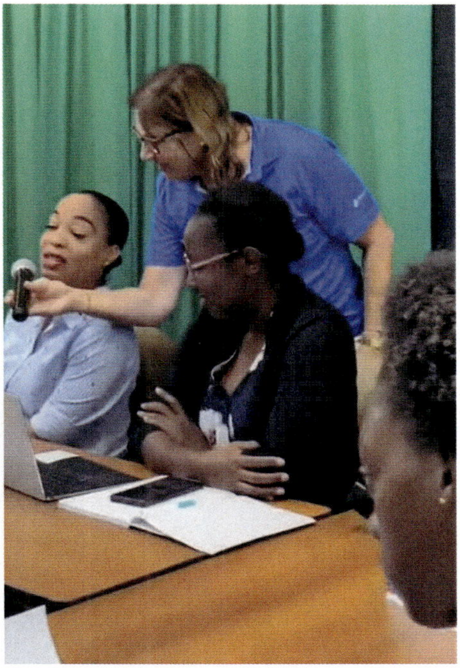

PAHF Event Management Workshop in Progress

Maureen Graig Rousseau and Laura Machiotti (PAHF) in discussion with some members of the LOC in January 2023.

Laura and Maureen also paid courtesy calls on JOA President, Christopher Samuda, and JOA General Secretary Ryan Foster, and Ms. Corinne Clarke (deputizing for the Acting General Manager) at the Sports Development Foundation. These meetings were both to update the JOA and SDF on the PAHF Events Management Workshop and to discuss, solicit, and solidify support for the tournament to be held in June of that year.

Meetings with JOA & Laura/Maureen
L-R: seated: President Christopher Samuda, CEO Ryan Foster (JOA), Maureen Graig Rousseau and Laura Machiotti (PAHF) and Fabian Stewart (JHF)

Meeting with SDF & Laura/Maureen
L-R: seated Maureen Graig Rousseau, Corinne Clark (SDF), Laura Machiotti and Fabian Stewart (JHF)

Internal Challenges

Solving Tournament Challenges

Unfortunately, several major challenges surfaced immediately. First, there was uncertainty on the side of the PAHF about the number of teams that were going to travel to Jamaica for the tournament based on the initial registration. This created a nightmare for completing a proper budget to seek funding and for understanding the scope of logistics and the effects on delivery timelines (recall the Project Constraint Triangle).

Second, we needed new Hockey5s boards, at great cost, for practice as well as for the competition. These boards would have to meet international specifications regarding the rebound of the ball as well as fit together to stay in place with increased impact from players. This was by no means an easy task and again required the attention of Dr. Campbell and Christopher Bowen, our now resident engineer and newly minted individual member (Surround yourself with those who know more than you.). So, we went to work, exploring several options, and finally creating an appropriate and approved solution slightly within budget after many conceptual iterations.

Third, our sponsorship efforts were not getting the traction or attention we had anticipated. While now cognizant that we required more professional assistance in the critical area of sponsorship, we encountered an unprecedented year for Jamaican team sports. The year 2023 was a very good year for Jamaica's sporting fraternity, in that, rugby, women's football, netball, lacrosse, and other sporting disciplines were doing well at the international level, hence creating greater competition for the sponsorship dollar. This fact was compounded by the economic risks and concomitant reduced cash outflow or spending by businesses due to the impending local government elections. The discretionary spending and financing of sports was, seemingly, constrained.

The team had to continuously cut, shave and find innovative ways to create solutions to accommodate the participants; for example, repurposing tents for team holding areas, borrowing stands to create the athletes' pavilion, and other initiatives.

Finally, Dr. Campbell, after very few meetings or no meetings of the LOC in February, candidly indicated to me that things were not moving well with the Committee. Leon Mitchell, the Chairman, was unavailable and this left the Committee members in limbo (Murphy's Law 101). In his usual direct manner, Carlton asked, "So when are you going to start leading the LOC?" This was a thought I had dreaded based on the other challenges being faced, including having to undertake the arrangements for our local male and female teams, which were not pleased with the focus and planning for auxiliary arrangements around their participation.

Understanding the context and the requirement for hands-on leadership, especially with time elapsing, the LOC was reassembled, and members were tasked around their specific competencies and experience. While this was not ideal, a few key members such as Carlton, Michael, Victor Tomlinson, and I, doubled, tripled and in some cases just executed critical operational tasks that were not being handled satisfactorily.

Pre-Tournament Team Tensions (Sports Psychology)

Pre-Meetings with TD Dr. Holt

Tensions were running high as the members of the national teams perceived what was really the focus of the few doing a lot to have the tournament get off the ground as a lack of attention being paid to them. Dr. Holt played a significant role as the part-time sports psychologist in trying to convey the sentiments of the coaching staff and players regarding their perception of a lack of preparation for their accommodation, transportation, and meals. After all, they were our national representatives. This situation created some very tense and at times explosive moments, discussions, and negotiations leading up to the tournament. The truth of the matter was that those who were tasked with the direct responsibility of our national teams (They know who they are ... love you and appreciate you ... but you know ...), just did not properly execute their assignments.

True leadership will always require the ultimate acceptance of responsibility, however unfair. So, adding more than 24 hours to the day, I worked on and negotiated a deal for accommodation with an entity on The UWI, Mona Campus, to satisfy both teams and managers but the trade-off was that the Federation would not provide the usual USD per diem based on the constraints being experienced. This is the kind of hard financial decision that sports managers and leaders need to make with the type of budgetary constraints we often have, as well as the perceived less-than-serious effort by the teams to seek sponsorship – a point that was communicated repeatedly to both teams.

However, after further discussions with Dr. Holt, representing the priorities of the teams, it was agreed eventually that the scarce resources would be allocated to a per diem (full meals and incidentals) with accommodation becoming the responsibility of the coaching staff and players. Smile* What a productive use of my limited available hours nearing the start of this major tournament!

The Difference of Gen X, Y and Z

It was not the ideal situation but, as President, and with the number of appeals in the public media for funding, the coaching staff and players were cognizant of the financial constraints leading up to the tournament. As usual, they wanted more, and as Millennials and Gen Zs, they really pushed the envelope based on their views on how they should be treated and what should be afforded them.

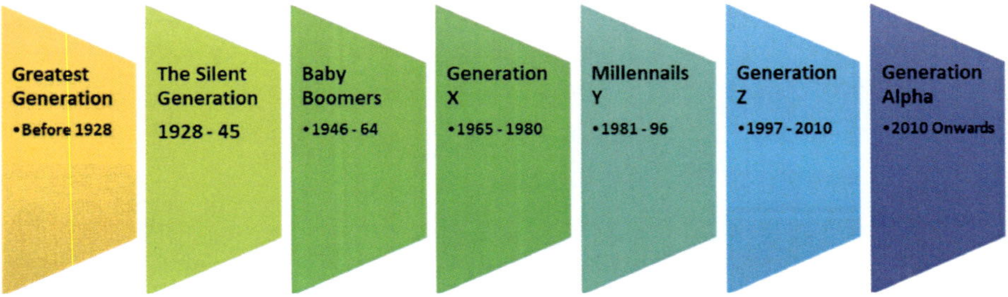

Figure 14 : The Different Generations

As the head of any organization, it is important to understand changes and dynamics in people based on their age group and how they were cultured to operate. Serious marketing and behavioural studies have been done over the years on the differences between the generations and it is a challenge that must be handled appropriately by sports administrators or risk fractures in the building of any federation or representational team. This was a point outlined by the earlier work and report done by Dr. Olivia Rose (Sports Psychologist) in 2018 with the national teams, where she consistently pointed out to me the differences between the needs of the current cadre of athletes versus the period of Boomers and Gen X. She also insisted on my participation (despite my reluctance) in sessions to better appreciate the differences, so that my management style could benefit.

Annazika Watkins, a colleague at the UWI, a trained social worker who works in the area of Gerontology, also provided vital insights and background concerning the 'nature and nurture' of Millennials (Gen Y) and Gen Zs and the impact on their psychological outlook. This, she explained, plays a significant role in critical thinking, impacts their attitude and commitment to things, such as setting goals for their own development in the sport. The recommendations that she provided were premised on her relationships with young adults and children. She advised that in order to bridge the gap between management/sports administrators and Gen Y and Z players, we needed to, among other things, learn to listen more – give them a voice; try to be less judgemental; and try to understand and be more facilitative of what they prioritize as their needs while discussing the Federation's constraints. She stressed that this must be done through effective communication which takes account of their current socio-economic circumstances and values.

Despite the recommendations and advice of Dr. Rose, Annazika Watkins and a few other stakeholders, Dr. Campbell and I, although we modified our approach, were reluctant to change most of our critical views on our Gen Y and Z players. This was probably because of our Gen X personality profiles. It could also have been the character traits of the younger generation in athletics such as the perceived sense of entitlement and lack of gratitude, observed by Michael Mignano, in a blog post on the website of the Association for Applied Sports Psychology on "Coaching Generation Z Athletes". His assessment of the positive and negative traits of Gen Z and Y are further highlighted in the section "Managing Crisis on the Road to Oman" (p. 165).

While we were cognizant of the differences in the attitudes between our generations, we most often pushed back on points raised by the younger folks, based on what we knew was an increased budgetary allocation towards the efforts of the National Teams (National Team Excellence) when compared to past efforts. We also observed what seemed to be a lack of appreciation for the Federation's genuine efforts to facilitate the needed activities/ demands of the national program and teams. Adding insult to injury was that in some instances, there seemed to be a lack of interest in assisting with and participating in fundraising efforts – funds the teams now required and, in some instances, demanded as a right!

Therefore, applying her sports psychology training, Dr. Holt became the conduit for the transfer and interpretation of messages from both parties, that is, national players and coaching staff and the JHF Board, and that seemed to allow us to better hear and communicate with each other.

Recognizing the overall tension, I had to further modify my approach to all within our fraternity at this important juncture. We had to ensure that all supporting stakeholders understood that much of what we wanted to achieve rested on the shoulders of our national representatives. On the other hand, I had to assure the national players that they were important and being heard; they were the tip of the spear for our battle, and were being accommodated as best as the JHF could.

In addition to Dr. Holt's work, this situation set the stage for true leadership lessons in our complex environment based on the Contingency Theory (Fielder 1963) regarding stakeholder values, communication of expected values, and the alignment of those expected values. This converged around the capacity of the power and influence of the leader. So, our vociferous discussions and disagreements coalesced around one particular point of communication – qualifying for the World Cup. Our disagreements subsided as we all knew we were focused on one goal at this time, winning enough games to participate in Oman.

… Was I sleeping? … Now this is interesting … just as I seemed to have found a good sleeping position … the announcement about preparing for landing … hmmm … I was really out ... Wonder if I was snoring … This lady is looking at me with a funny smile ...

External Challenges

Addition of More Teams for the Qualifiers

Understanding Murphy's Law is understanding sports management and planning. Being a student of Murphy's Law College, it didn't surprise me when a major challenge suddenly faced our planning for the Pan Am Qualifier, requiring serious negotiation and planning around the constraints triangle.

After creating a budget for possibly 5 teams per gender based on early interests registered by our discussions with PAHF, our numbers suddenly increased to the possibility of approximately 9 to 10 teams per gender. This created a nightmare scenario for our planning. It exponentially increased our budget to accommodate all the requirements based on our signed hosting agreement. The numbers significantly increased our costs, predominantly for infrastructure and logistics, accommodation, and other auxiliary requirements such as mandatory hydration. As mentioned in Chapter 2, it also affected the timelines and scope of Work Based Packages (WBS).

This situation prompted the request for a serious meeting with the Minister of Sport for a reconsideration of the original sum that was proposed for supporting the venture. Despite the significant increase in the new budget for the tournament, we were confident in our budgetary construct (Chapter Three, Financial Sustainability: Budgeting Process), especially the costs associated with the input variables, and could easily justify our expenditure and cash outflows based on new assumptions for teams being hosted.

Meeting with Minister Grange

Our objective was simple: properly present our case for additional funding to efficiently host the event. I was almost out the door in my usual casual outfit because I like to be comfortable. My wife, the perennial government bureaucrat, asked me, "Is today your meeting? And is that the way you dressed to meet the Minister? Really!" Enough said. I quickly returned to my room and assumed a more corporate mindset in my approach (something I am quite capable of doing!). So, did Dr. Campbell when he enquired about my mode of dress for the meeting and I repeated my wife's loud condemnation regarding my choice of attire for this critical meeting with our Minister.

Our meeting was late Friday morning, March 14, 2023, at the Ministry. The Minister was attentive to our presentation. She skilfully analyzed our increases and variances from the original budget that was submitted. While she was dissecting our budget with Suzzette Irvin-Ison, Director of Sport in the Ministry, probing questions were asked which we answered factually and confidently. In short, this was the first event of its kind and PAHF was hopeful of entries and interest but not sure of the confirmations that informed the development of a more conservative budget. Once it became clear that we were going to have many more teams than originally budgeted and the ramifications this would have on the constraint triangle, the Minister was clearer on our request for additional funding and, therefore, more receptive.

Presentation Meeting with Minister Grange and Suzette Ison Director of Sport regarding Hockey5s Qualifier at the Ministry of Sport

Surprisingly, notwithstanding Minister Grange's extensive portfolio and time constraints and challenges (that is, Minister for Gender, Culture, Entertainment and Sport), we had a full-length meeting with her incorporating very open and practical discussions on the tournament regarding income generation and sponsorship. However, I doubt we could forget her comments about the approach of our presentation, which she stated was similar to how Pastor Gino Jennings (whom she said was me) and his main pastor on stage (Dr. Campbell) operated, where the latter answered questions and echoed agreement with the main points made by Pastor Jennings. On that point, we had a good laugh!

Discussing Budgetary Increase with Minister Grange at the Ministry of Sport

The experienced and savvy Minister Grange, while now more understanding of the complexities, did not commit to the percentage increase in funding that was being requested but gave a slight indication that an addition to the original sum committed would be more favourably considered.

Although we didn't leave the meeting with assurance, we would get the four loaves of bread we so badly wanted, we were given an indication of a possible one-and-a-half loaves commitment. This meant a further restructuring and 'juggling' of our budgetary expenditure while ensuring we satisfied the international requirements for the tournament. Dear Lord, more fights with Carlton, Ms. Daisy's One Son, who was hell-bent on satisfying all the international obligations as best as possible. After having qualified, we thanked the Minister with, albeit belatedly, a gift of a journey board for her help and support as well as that of her team in making the Road to Oman a reality.

Journey Board Presented to Minister

Well, well, well ... this airport seems huge! Going through immigration now ... Where do I go to find the Turkish Airline Agent … not much English but give instructions on paper to find the counter … ok … Let's start walking …

Lighting the Road to Oman

Upgrading to LED Lights at the Facility

Incorporated in our strategic planning process under National Leagues and Tournament was the desire to install LED lights for the facility. These types of lights would allow for flexibility in scheduling games and training, as well as offer a strategy to mitigate against climate change due to increasing day time temperatures.

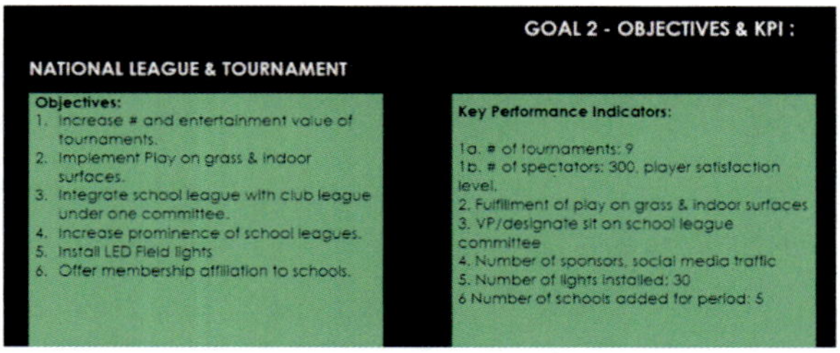
GOAL 2 - OBJECTIVES & KPI :

NATIONAL LEAGUE & TOURNAMENT

Objectives:	Key Performance Indicators:
1. Increase # and entertainment value of tournaments. 2. Implement Play on grass & indoor surfaces. 3. Integrate school league with club league under one committee. 4. Increase prominence of school leagues. 5. Install LED Field lights 6. Offer membership affiliation to schools.	1a. # of tournaments: 9 1b. # of spectators: 300, player satisfaction level. 2. Fulfilment of play on grass & indoor surfaces 3. VP/designate sit on school league committee 4. Number of sponsors, social media traffic 5. Number of lights installed: 30 6 Number of schools added for period: 5

Figure 15: Extracts from the JHF Strategic Plan, Goal 2 - Objectives & KPIs: National League and Tournament (Source: Jamaica Hockey Federation Strategic Plan, 2018)

However, the more significant reason was the requirement for regional level games.

Bearing this in mind, the JHF owes Dr. Carlton Campbell a debt of gratitude for the acquisition, by way of donation, and installation of new LED lights at the Mona astro turf. To say Carlton has taken the development and maintenance of the JHF premises seriously is an understatement. His actions single-handedly allowed for fixtures to have games late into the evening and nights, especially with the increased number of teams. The new lights also satisfied the minimum 500 lumen requirements by (FIH/PAHF) for night games.

Workmen Removing the Old Lights and Lighting fixtures

Now, Carlton had worked his magic and, through a private donation, secured the new state-of-the-art LED lights that were installed a few weeks before the start of the tournament. It would be remiss of me not to mention the Sports Development Foundation and the Jamaica Olympic Association for also assisting with the importation and installation of the lights at the facility.

Drone Comparison of Difference in Lumen between New and Old Lights at the Turf

Hockey5s training session under the new lights

The highly sophisticated system provided and installed by David Darling and his team from Power Lighting and Communication gave Dr. Campbell, or any manager of the facility, the ability to remotely turn on and off the lights, which was excellent for time and cost management. LED are low energy so our energy bills were also reduced significantly.

A quick comparative cost estimate of the electricity expenditure for hosting the CAC Games Qualifiers in 2017 and the Hockey5s World Cup Qualifiers provides a good cost-benefit analysis. In 2017, we used the lights that we had to support the required lumen for games ending in the evenings as most games were played in daylight. So, for only three evenings for approximately 2 hours per day, the electricity cost based on our bill was estimated to be JMD120K (1 US Dollar = 128.31 JMD). In contrast, we spent an estimated JMD28K (1 US Dollar = 150.80 JMD) for a full week of competition, utilizing the LED lights for approximately 4 to 5 hours per night for about 2 weeks, for practice and night games.

Critical Areas for the Regional Tournament

Engagement of Transportation and Logistics Service

The area of transportation is critical for tournaments, and we had some interesting logistical situations to maneuver. Mr. Noel Williams, President of the Jamaica Union of Travellers Association (JUTA), was extremely helpful and cooperative. He worked with the JHF to plan the logistics and transportation. He modified the original thought of just engaging the buses for trips rather than the shuttle service. Based on the multiple games per day, the movement to and from the hotels to the venue required a rework of the approach that we had envisioned. The JOA also assisted in the area of transportation by providing a much-needed bus designated for the officials.

Interestingly, all the LOC members volunteered and pitched in where necessary, especially with intermediate transportation, especially for special requests by officials (Victor Tomlinson, Richard Shaw, Valerie Hall, and Richard Wisdom). Dr. Campbell and I pitched in and used our vehicles as delivery trucks for hydration, snacks, ice, and any sundries or other commodities required.

Medical Preparation

Dr. Patrice Simmonds-Brooks and her medical team were also critical to the preparation and the event, as well as the Sports Medicine Association of Jamaica and their team of volunteers who covered the event. Dr. Simmonds-Brooks assisted the JHF in understanding the medical requirements for the tournament along with providing a fully equipped ambulance. While two ambulances were probably required, Dr. Brooks and her team implemented a good transfer system with available vehicles (my truck) for a cost-effective medical operation that provided excellent service. In fact, based on the PAHF Technical Director's report for the tournament, the medical apparatus was given the highest score.

As the medical emergency vehicle of choice based on the need for the ambulance for more serious injuries, I recall my assignment was to take a Paraguayan player (I think with a broken finger or hand) to the Andrews Memorial Hospital, a private hospital about 20–25 minutes away from the field, depending on traffic. Dr. Simmonds-Brooks indicated the need for an x-ray at a facility where it could be done faster than at the Emergency Room (ER) at the University Hospital of the West Indies (UHWI), the designated tournament hospital.

Patricia Niella, President of Paraguay Hockey accompanied us to the hospital and was holding onto the vehicle's grab handles for dear life while we rushed to the hospital. Unable to speak much English, her sighs and body language were enough for me to see the need to consistently reassure her that we wouldn't have an accident. I could see the nervous smile and heard the anxious sounds. Well, I don't speak Spanish, but I do speak nervous!

Hockey5s Pitch Preparation

While I have only pointed out a few examples of services provided by the members of my hockey family, there are many more instances of the village coming together to make the Road to Oman become a reality. Regarding surface preparation, for example, we have to acknowledge the work of Audrey Gaynor, Michelle Thompson, and Richard 'Buju' Pollock on the preparation of the Hockey5s pitch before and throughout the tournament. I remember Audrey with the leaf blower and Michelle sweeping and removing excess sand from the surface. They also aided with fixing the boards and ensuring the pitch was ready for play. Michelle Thompson also became an aggressive guardian of the ice box and hydration supplies, ensuring proper distribution to all teams and officials. Many of our dysfunctional family members assisted in one way or the other and, to them, I am eternally grateful.

Digital Preparation

The office container pod for hosting the broadcasters and streaming service were in place, an area agreed to have a positive impact on the visibility of the tournament. The social media space, marshalled by Director Panton, was in full motion. There were advertisements on social media, including an infomercial done by Simon Preston, 876Stream leading up to the tournament. This was also complemented by video advertisements appearing across Kingston on strategic digital boards.

Our partnerships with marketing sponsors and government agencies, such as the Jamaica Tourist Board and Sports Development Foundation, provided additional free-to-air access, especially via website links to our tournament page. In addition to these avenues, the interviews on podcasts as well as internal interviews linked to the JHF's social media platforms (Instagram and Twitter [now X]) certainly provided good coverage utilizing, shall we say, a very economical marketing budget. Information about the tournament certainly made the circuit.

The Volunteer Army

A serious but underappreciated area in major events of this nature is the army of volunteers who work in every area of the tournament. Andrea Hoo Thomas created a good army from her recruitment efforts. They were extremely helpful as ball boys and girls, team liaisons, technical officials, as runners restocking the hydration drums and helping in so many other areas.

Jamaica has always been known for its hospitality but the volunteers as entertainment coordinators really had all the visitors attempting the latest dance moves and having a terrific time. Their contribution was well appreciated as they are a major part of the success of the tournament.

The Team of Volunteers Keeping the Vibes

Volunteers interacting with Players & Coaches

Now it's that time! We have tested, set up, and made changes, and as the silence dawns on the facility, we slowly make our way away from the expectant looking setup at the field for the opening day of the first Pan Am World Cup Hockey5s Qualifier. It seems that, again, we have pulled the rabbit from the hat!

Time for the Tournament!

What the … these instructions are taking me around in a circle … What? Left after you pass this restaurant? What left? …. Look for stairs ... but those were before the other instruction … I am now tired and confused walking through what seems to be a big high-end mall …. Let me ask this guy …

Test Runs for the Road to Oman

Teams arrived early so that we were able to have a few dress rehearsals concerning transportation. The teams, having been provided with a few hotel options, stayed at the Courtleigh Hotel, The UWI Mona Campus (Elsa Leo-Rhynie Hall (also known as Towers) and 138 Student Living), Liguanea Club, and the Four Seasons Hotel. The officials were housed at the Four Seasons. As is customary with a major tournament in our Pan Am region, bulletins were circulated to all teams to provide information about the island and proposed accommodation. Of course, we had questions arising from some of the teams and I had to rely on a former co-worker, Deidre-Ann Burrell, to handle communication with teams that needed responses in Spanish. She was especially helpful in assisting our Spanish-speaking teams with securing their accommodation.

In our test runs, we saw the challenges early in the game with pitch access arrangements for the respective teams, and getting them to and from the venue as other teams wanted to be picked up. I recall Michelle Thompson, Ricardo Panton and I had to run a shuttle service to The UWI, Mona Campus (5 minutes away from the pitch) to facilitate ease of movement for the teams, especially the team from Panama.

So, while the scattered locations proved a bit challenging, thanks to the help of Noel Williams, Richard Wisdom, and Victor Tomlinson (especially Victor), there were no delayed games and minimal complaints about the transportation service. More importantly, there were no complications associated with the arrival and departure of the teams.

Uruguay Arrives in Montego Bay

Dana's Girls from Uruguay had made arrangements that landed them in Montego Bay for a tournament in Kingston – 3+ hours by road, 188+ km away.

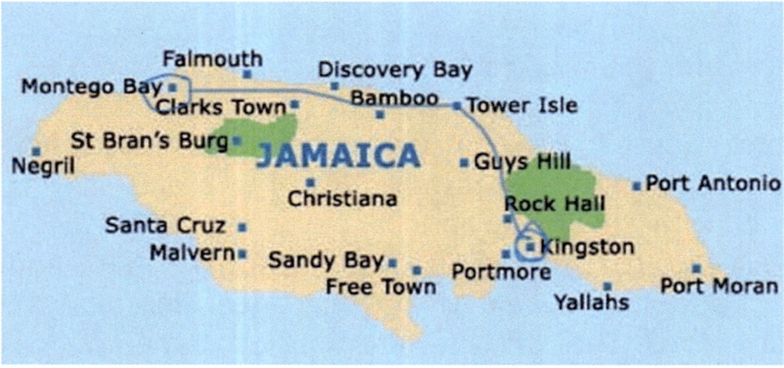

Figure 16: Map of Jamaica showing the distance between Montego Bay and Kingston
Source: http://www.world-guides.com/latin-america/jamaica/ .

How the hell! But no worries, we had to quickly request the intervention of Noel Williams from JUTA to work his magic and have the team transported quickly to Kingston very soon after their arrival.

Technical Official Pre-Tournament Checks

The advance team of officials arrived and checked everything from a pin to an anchor. Laura and Carlton accommodated last-minute details in order to get things just right for the officials. Rene Zelkin, the PAHF Technical Director, was simply a gift from the gods in this process.

Rene Zelkin, PAHF Technical Director

We worked assiduously through most issues and challenges with a level of understanding that was very well appreciated, from simple administrative issues to major issues of rain delays and security. She was demanding but also sought to facilitate solutions to the issues or challenges based on our circumstances and situation. I was also impressed with her decision making, especially regarding keeping the tournament moving after rain delays. And trust me, we did have some rain that week!

But we also had other unfortunate issues to quickly address. For anyone in the sports administration arena, your ultimate aim is achieving an incident-free tournament. Unfortunately, Murphy's Law is always going to be in effect. For us, believe it or not, one of those incidents was one, or more than one suspected case of chickenpox, unreported or detected by the traveling party, which had to be swiftly and quietly managed on the medical side to reduce exposure to the other participants.

There were other issues such as the language barrier and executing urgent requests from participants. However, having professionals like Deidre-Ann Burrell, my unofficial interpreter for both Spanish and French (thank you Deidre), Dr. Brooks, and staff from the Sports Medicine Association was a tremendous help.

Good technical officials with a sense of humor and flexibility in the midst of the organized chaos helps to reduce the stress associated with these tournaments and add a little bit of fun to the occasion. Take, for example, the screenshot of Susan Gomes, Umpires Manager for the tournament and a riot of a woman, and teacher of the rules of the game. We were on a video call jokingly telling Maureen Craig-Rousseau in Trinidad that she needed to return in person to collect the item she left behind on her last visit (the PAHF event management training course) to the island, as Susan was not a courier. As every sporting administrator knows, the temperature can get really turned up when countries are competing in a regional tournament.

Video Message to Maureen in Trinidad from Susan Gomes

Expectations for the Road to Oman

Discussions with the Dr. Holt (TD), and Henlon, the Coach

As we drew closer to the tournament, I grew to respect the coaching staff even more, especially the TD, despite some challenges. Yes, I knew of personality issues and challenges but I prioritized having the capabilities we had lacked for several previous tournaments (No disrespect is intended to other past coaches by this statement.). There was a deficit in the utility and application of modern field hockey IQ skills (It's a new game requiring new thinking and investment in learning.). This had been nurtured throughout the development of the Elite Coaching Program.

Now, for those that may not be around Dr. Holt and who are unfamiliar with her hockey game knowledge and predictions, to use Malcolm Gladwell's explanation of thin slicing in Blink, she has an extremely high hockey IQ and probably spends more hours than any current person in our Federation as a student of the game, particularly tactically.

Now before my harsh Jamaican critics and detractors who cannot appreciate a queen in her own country start to push back, check the history of her winning record – club and country – and her hockey resume, and then let us have a conversation.
Let me state this clearly: having known Michelle Holt, I think from her playing days, and being around field hockey for a seriously long time, she is more correct on various field hockey determinations than most people that I have been aware of. But she has a few (thank goodness) spectacular perceptions at times associated with the game that, in my view, are simply opposite to logic ... just plain wrong! I guess there is just a thin line between genius and insanity.

However, calls made by both Michelle and Henlon in winning the CAC Games Qualifiers in Bermuda with that young inexperienced team, in spite of the limited preparation time over the period of the COVID-19 pandemic, high number of uncapped players, and the balls of steel decisions that I would not make as a coach, made me a little more than respectful of their coaching methods and tactical analysis of the games.

So, when I asked Michelle and Henlon about our chances in the quiet moments, both responded that we were going to Oman! As usual, despite wanting the result, my cautious personality thought, as team leaders you have to demonstrate the belief for others to follow. Their views were: for the Men – beat this team, possibly lose here, recover here, and beat this team and we are in! For the Women – beat this team, if not, the road becomes harder.

As I delved a little deeper and was confronted with their more in-depth analysis of the teams present, those absent, and our strengths and weaknesses relative to our opponents along with other historical information, they both made me a little more quietly optimistic about our chances to travel the Road to Oman. Imagine, Jamaica field hockey in their first World Cup Competition for the FIH! A resounding validation for the strategic direction of the past 7 years, the paradigm shift, and strategic planning.

Whoever wrote those instructions in the Istanbul airport … We are not friends. Now, finally at the Turkish Airlines ticketing agent … more confusion … Where does this line start?

Ah ha! I am not the only person here with anger management challenges. Fellow at the counter is loud as hell … missed his connection to England coming from Malaysia, causing him what seems like another 24-hour layover, with a suggestion of being rerouted with over 8 hours flying time and potential delays … or …

Summary

The strategic planning by the PAHF Board of the Events Management Workshop allowed early discussion on the tournament requirements but also allowed PAHF representatives to officially support the tournaments with important courtesy calls on our sporting partners, particularly the JOA and SDF.

Internal and external challenges and the effects on the Triple Constraint Triangle for the tournament were also outlined in this chapter. The solutions to challenges underscore the leadership capabilities (understanding the Contingency and Situational

Theories) and competencies within the JHF but, more importantly, our grasp of finance and the ability to make the necessary and hard decisions.

The assistance of key players to ensure high standards in healthcare, transportation, logistics, communication, volunteer and facilities management were crucial areas discussed and managed for the preparation work for the tournament. The contingency plans put in place, that is, private medical transportation as well as assistance with scheduling and ensuring adequate preparation for the tournament within the budgetary constraints, were just a few solutions highlighted for the tournament.

The installation of the LED lights for the tournament under the Major Tournament or Tournaments and Leagues Strategic Objective/Pillar was also featured because of its significant impact on efficiently hosting the tournament.

From the technical team's pre-checks and test runs to various systems and discussions on expectations with Jamaica's TD and Coach, it was now time for the tournament.

Chapter Six:
The Tournament

The inaugural Pan Am Hockey5s World Cup Qualifier was hosted at the Mona Hockey Turf in Kingston, Jamaica, June 4–11, 2023. Confirmed for the tournament were 8 teams on the Men's side and 9 on the Women's. With all teams in the island and settled in, follow along for a day-by-day synopsis of the matches and activities surrounding the tournament up to the closing ceremonies.

Men	Women
JAM – Jamaica	JAM – Jamaica
GUA – Guatemala	GUA – Guatemala
PAN – Panama	PAN – Panama
TTO – Trinidad and Tobago	TTO – Trinidad and Tobago
CRC – Costa Rica	CRC – Costa Rica
USA – United States	USA – United States
PAR – Paraguay	PAR – Paraguay
PUR – Puerto Rico	URU – Uruguay
	BRA – Brazil

Table 1: Final Pan Am Hockey5s World Cup Qualifier Participating Teams (Males/Females)

With well over 250 players and coaches and 25 officials visiting the island from over 15 countries, we were set to start the games.

It's Almost Go Time!

The technical team arrived at the venue at approximately 10:00 a.m. for setup, going through from a pin to an anchor. Then a concern on the pitch at the goals for which everyone seemed serious about finding a quick solution. Holy crap! More work needed on the pitch and goal area before the start of the games! Why were these things not seen earlier in the inspections from Friday and Saturday?

There was an issue with the proper pinning of the goal nets but, more seriously, the manner in which the rubber inside the goal box jutted out from inside of the post. This could cause a shot to rebound or deflect goal scoring opportunities. So, Rene Zelkin, the PAHF TD, Susan, the Umpires Manager, along with a few other officials, tried to cut this thick, black conveyor belt rubber with a knife to eliminate the potential issue. Talk about mission impossible! But we certainly gave it a go on all fours. Then the brilliant idea of just removing the screws and taking the darn thing out was proposed. It worked for a bit, then there was more stubborn resistance from bent and broken screws. I will never forget the actions of David Darling to save the day! He was working to ensure there was adequate power to the light poles and proper voltage to the Office Container Modules (PODs) housing for the commentators' booth and equipment for the live streaming, which was the domain of Nani El Barri, PAHF Technical and Communications Officer. He saw us trying to rectify anomalies in the goal boxes. He came over after realizing our fruitless efforts with a knife, then a hammer, to do a really difficult task, and provided us with his power tool to cut the rubber and execute the job in mere minutes. Problem solved!

Carlton and his team, plus the new volunteers, ran through the essentials: water, tents, electronic system, FIH Tournament Management System (TMS), wi-fi, ball boys, benches, boards corrected, scissors jack in place for video-recording of games, our clock that can't be seen in the daylight (damn), sound system check (national anthems, etc.), and the teams, coaching staff and umpires, and buses. Then we started again … ice check, tickets for the gate, radios … damn the radios weren't charged last night …

Without much fanfare, at 1:00 p.m, Sunday, June 4, 2023, Paraguay and Costa Rica got the tournament on the way. Interestingly enough, some countries didn't bring the Olympic Games version of their anthem, so a few national anthems required a little patience before the start of the game.

Well, finally routed to Dubai for another 4 hrs 30 mins … then 3 or 4 hours in-transit, en route to Muscat on Oman Air … another 1 hr 30 mins … What is the alternative? The same flight tomorrow night! Will my checked luggage arrive with me in Muscat …? Oh yes! Sure, Sir! Hmmmm … please hurry, you have an hour to check in

The Competition Gets Underway

Day 1: Good Start for the Competition, but not for Team Jamaica

The results of the tournament are posted on the FIH website at: https://www.fih.hockey/events/hockey-5s-pan-am/schedule-fixtures-results. There you will be able to have a more in-depth look at the games. But focusing on the Road to Oman, Jamaica had a fair start for the Men but a fall against Trinidad in their Women's group meant an even harder climb in the competition.

Match Day 1: Sunday, June 4 – Rough Start https://www.fih.hockey/events/hockey-5s-pan-am/schedule-fixtures-results

While ensuring everything was moving ahead according to plan, I was thinking about how to manage the threat of rain though, oddly enough, we had brilliant sunshine for the start of the tournament. Our Women's team got off to a stumble to Trinidad (TTO), our Caribbean rivals. While our Men put up a good show, they unluckily lost 4:2 to the USA.

Exhausted, our small team did our debriefing, planned for Day 2, and solved a few requests. I recall getting home on pure adrenalin and just sitting on the settee, in a daze.

The Excel Miscalculation (A Happy and Sad Moment)

While I have heard of Excel issues from my accounting friends, experience is, indeed, the greatest teacher. When you host a PAHF tournament, the host is responsible for the cost of accommodation, meals, and per diem for the officials. The number of officials and days they are working at the tournament therefore dictates directly the amount to be budgeted.

Here is some more crazy Law 101 in Murphy's Law College. We utilized an Excel spreadsheet provided by PAHF as an example for the expeditious calculation of per diem. So, there I was reviewing and providing the agreed US dollars for per diem to a puzzled looking Laura Macchiotti, Event Coordinator. She calculated and recalculated and then asked me, smiling, in a very soft voice, "Fabian, why are you giving me so much money?" I was too tired for jokes, so I looked at Laura, puzzled, and quickly produced my laptop with the calculations.

We then both reviewed and saw the formula error in the Excel spreadsheet! I was happy and sad at the same time (didn't know that could happen) – happy for a significant reduction in our budget but sad because I knew my perceived surplus from this error was already spent on other payments and debts racked up for the tournament.

Monday, June 5: Match Day 2 – Morning Session
https://www.fih.hockey/events/hockey-5s-pan-am/schedule-fixtures-results

A better day for Jamaica; our Women played to a draw with Brazil. Brazil was uncertain of making the tournament but I appreciated the effort that they took to participate.

Jamaica Men, on the other hand, fared better, beating Panama, so I promised Ademir Montenegro Cortes, my fellow PAHF Board Member, some Jamaican rum.

Tuesday, June: Match Day 3 – Morning Session
https://www.fih.hockey/events/hockey-5s-pan-am/schedule-fixtures-results

Jamaica Men also clipped Puerto Rico 3 to 2 in the evening game. I can't remember seeing much of that game, for some reason. On the other hand, our Women were hammered against Team Uruguay. Uruguay demonstrated their international caliber and why they were considered a favorite for the tournament.

The win was good for the Men as it buoyed the spirits of the Jamaican camp. And it was also good for them going into the rest day on Wednesday 7.

Wednesday, June 7: No Rest for the Administrators

The rest day gave my LOC team the opportunity to recalibrate and address all the challenges and issues that we had encountered. This included the movement of things like ice, water and rehydration fluids for all essential areas, the sound system, food, volunteers and other matters required by the technical and visiting teams. The brief respite also offered an opportunity for Carlton and his ground staff to handle the necessary sweeping of the turf, repairs and other maintenance work. I also remember us still recalculating and moving cash around to ensure that our financial obligations were being met or at least partially met.

Thursday, June 8: Match Day 4 – Women Crossover
https://www.fih.hockey/events/hockey-5s-pan-am/schedule-fixtures-results
The Jamaica Women beat Guatemala 1:0 to cement their rematch

with Brazil for the 5th and 6th positions.

Again, despite the win, the performance of our Women was a little disappointing. I knew that the inconsistency of the players in general probably drove Coach Nicole Bradshaw, TD Michelle Holt and her coaching staff crazy, as there were simple moments of brilliance followed by moments of 'what the hell'.

Friday, June 9: Match Day 5 – Crossovers Morning Men https://www.fih.hockey/events/hockey-5s-pan-am/schedule-fixtures-results

Wow, that was a close one!

While I felt that the Jamaica Men should have the better of Guatemala based on our competition history, it was clear that Guatemala did not view themselves as minions to Jamaica. Yet again, I thought some simple inconsistencies within the play of the Jamaican Men made this crossover game much more exciting than we wanted it to be, ending in a tie and going to a shootout, where I have seen the best of players crack under pressure. But it seemed the desire to make history propelled us to a good shootout series, taking us past Guatemala to a semi-final berth with our neighbors Trinidad and Tobago.

... On the flight to Dubai ... Hmmm this isn't bad ... not too full, more space for the knees ... more food ... another movie ... but ... feeling tired so let me try to get some rest ...

Friday, June 9: Match Day 5 – Crossovers Evening Game https://www.fih.hockey/events/hockey-5s-pan-am/schedule-fixtures-results

Having squeezed past Guatemala by way of a nerve-racking shootout, I suspected that we entered the game with TTO wishing for the best but fully understanding the caliber of players our Caribbean neighbors were bringing to the party. They had invested more strategically in their players' development, with many getting the opportunity to play in Europe at a significantly higher level of the sport than our region has to offer.

Our thoughts of a Jamaican upset quickly vanished as a rampant TTO demonstrated why their eventual 8th place finish in the Hockey5s World Cup and higher FIH ranking were justified. Our dreams of getting on the Road to Oman had to wait another day. But the Men were focused and ready for the opportunity. At this game, I recalled my discussions with Coach Henlon and TD Dr. Holt: "Win here, lose here, but win here and we are in!"

Tragedy along the Road to Oman

On Saturday, June 10, I was in my office going over the numbers and ensuring that we were in fact accounting for all our expenditure. My Treasurer had been MIA with good reason – his wife was terminally ill. So, I had to put my postgraduate degree in finance to work.

Glen Patrick was calling me. "Yes, Glen!" I recall feeling a chill down my spine when he solemnly asked, "Have you heard?" He continued in my silence, "Blake Roper was in an accident and died last night!" Stunned into further silence, my exhaustion was replaced immediately with anguish, remorse, disbelief, and utter grief. "Are you still there?" Glen asked, and, losing the fight to hold back tears, I responded, "I was just with the man a few hours ago at the hockey field and he said he was tired! But he was ensuring we got the flag poles we needed and was also seeing to the setting up of a tent in the athlete's area." His untimely death and the possibility that I (we) added to his exhaustion still pains my heart to this day.

Our attempts to access flag poles from the military through the regular channels via a letter asking for flag poles and a tent had failed. I reached out to Blake in May and he responded that he was getting back to Jamaica on June 1. We communicated again on June 6 about the tent and he indicated that he heard that we had requested some flag poles as well.

Interestingly, I was at the field with Lt. Col. (Ret'd) D.C. Lobban and Lt. Col. Ret'd Roderick Rowe, looking over the arrangements and setup for the next day of the tournament. We were sitting in our usual VIP area and Bar above the clubhouse setup by Sandra Blair and her team. Not having any flag poles, we did what we had seen done in other countries, and that was to put the flags on the fence.

Flags on the Fence JHF

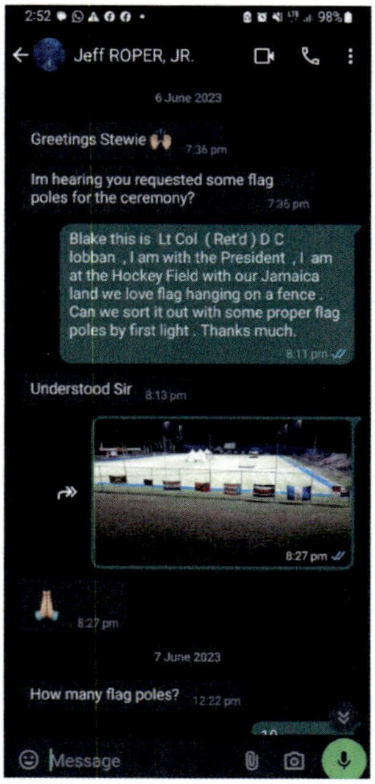

This struck a nerve with both military men, with Lt. Col. (Ret'd) D.C. Lobban using my phone to send a WhatsApp message to Blake.

Such was the dependability and respect that we had become accustomed to from Blake. I sometimes remark that the leaves do not fall far from the tree, as we became accustomed to help from his father, Col. Ret'd. Geoffery Roper, when preparing for events. I had the privilege of playing alongside his father on the Jamaica National Team in the 1990s. In some instances, because of Geoffrey's superior fitness, you felt he was playing for all of us that operated in the midfield, and knew if you made a mistake or struggled to get back in position, you would simply see the area covered by Mr. Dependable.

Blake loved hockey and would have easily made any national and junior national team. But his first love was military service and that took him away from the game and the island for a while. But upon his return, we had a few conversations over the years where he promised to re-engage with the Federation to assist with our development and connection to the Jamaica Defence Force (JDF), the patron of the sport in Jamaica.

Blake seemed to be a mirror of his father's traits (except the early days of PHAT THURSDAYZ Masters hockey game when he was the younger competitor). Both Ropers had to be on opposing teams. Driven by their exceedingly competitive nature, some angry but respectful disagreements on foul calls and other plays took place. Both always operated with the same high standard, integrity, and serious commitment to deliverables. They both earned my respect!

He was at the field on the night of June 9 and we spoke. He remarked that we had received the flag poles and he also got us a 20ft x 20ft tent to assist with coverage in the athletes' pavilion. We were in real need of this coverage as rain, and at times intense sunshine, made the area uncomfortable.

Dr. Holt also recalled speaking to him while he assisted with instructions to the soldiers who were setting up the tent at the field. She recalled his mention of being exhausted but he was more interested in knowing about the progress and chances of the teams in the Qualifier.

Needing to demonstrate our loss at the tournament, upon the request of the team, I submitted a request to FIH to allow the teams to wear a black appendage to their kits to signify the loss. This was approved.

The Mark of Respect (Incorrect Protocol)

In my attempt to show respect for our fallen member, I attempted to fly the Jamaican flag at half-mast for a day. This action had to be quickly reversed when word came from an individual associated with our Ministry of Foreign Affairs about the appropriate observance of the protocols for this action.

This would have included the time-consuming task of preparing a specific letter to the Minister of Foreign Affairs outlining the reason for the request and awaiting a formal response on the internal and external discussions to facilitate the formal approval of the action to be taken, especially with flags from other countries also mounted in the same venue.

L: Flag flown at half-mast (without regard to protocol) to mourn the death of our member, Captain Blake Roper

The irony of life is that Blake Roper was a person in the military, who acted on principles, regulations and protocols. He was instrumental in getting the flag poles upon which we tried to demonstrate our heartfelt loss and respect for him. By doing so without the proper permission to signal our deep and immediate sorrow, we ran the risk of defiling the very high principles he stood for.

I knew and recognized that we were all a bit dazed but had to carry on, as we knew he would have wanted. The rest of the tournament was bittersweet and the pain of his loss was only dulled by the exhaustion associated with the non-stop activities associated with hosting the tournament.

R: Flag corrected later that day based on required protocols for flying the Jamaican flag at half-mast.

Captain Blake James Roper
February 28, 1992 - June 10, 2023

Rest In Peace

Saturday, June 10: Match Day 6 – Female Finals

Jamaica Placed 5th

Jamaica Hockey5s Team Women

In my opinion, the Women's team had performed a little lower than anticipated but they certainly came back well and fully deserved their 5th place in the competition. Seeming to get better with each game, their 3:1 beating of my sentimental team, Brazil, in a convincing manner, was an indication of the inconsistencies that I think should have driven Coach Nicole Bradshaw and her coaching staff absolutely crazy.

Pablo's Paraguay Defeat Fido's TTO Girls

I certainly had mixed feelings about Paraguay's defeat of Trinidad and Tobago to earn the bronze medal and a trip to Oman. Glen 'Fido' Francis and the T&T girls were Caribbean and despite our extensive rivalry, Jamaica Hockey will automatically root for the next Caribbean team, no matter what. We are neighbors and one Caribbean. Besides, they were playing good hockey and seemed destined to beat Paraguay. However, Paraguay was being coached by Pablo Mendoza, who was, and who would have been further involved in the Jamaican development program, possibly

Coaching Jamaica, had it not been for the pandemic. He was also instrumental in the recommendation of Devaughn Henlon as the best prospect of all in his sessions for head coach of Jamaica. He also provided continued guidance to Jamaica on our development pathways.

Team Paraguay

Women's Finals – A Masterclass

The Women's final between the USA and Uruguay was a masterclass in international Hockey5s with skill, grit, and determination on full display throughout the match. Despite an excellent comeback with the 2 goals from Piazza Camila, it seemed the injury to Vilar Manuela (Player of the Tournament) aided the outcome of the match. While both teams fought to the bitter end, the USA managed to prevail in the shootout. Excellent game!

Team Uruguay

Vilar Manuela, Player of the Tournament award, presented by Victor Tomlinson

I was happy to see Abby Burnett from Team USA participating in the finals, having been one of my medical emergencies who had to go to the University Hospital of the West Indies (UHWI) emergency room with a broken nose.

Abby Burnett

The Closing Ceremony for the Women
(Murphy Strikes Again?)

It was time for the closing ceremony for females, and everything had been organized by Laura Macchiotte and Trisha Barber. Everything was running smoothly despite Laura's need for speed in executing the program and distribution of the medals – not a cultural norm in the Caribbean. We were through with the brief speeches and medals were awarded. The event proceeded according to plan. President 'Coco' Budeisky was about to present the medals and winning trophy to the USA and then ... the unimaginable happened. Thank God, we had completed about 80% of the program.

Team USA Women Champions

All the lights went out! For a second, I shook my head, thinking this couldn't be real and happening again. I felt a little relieved to learn that it was an unexpected blackout on a major grid across Kingston and St. Andrew. Interestingly, Carlton and I were having the same discussion before and throughout the tournament about the installation of a backup generator for the lights. However, these are the tough but necessary financial decisions that needed to be made, and I had to consider other uses for the JMD 500,000 expense to mitigate the risk of a power outage.

President Coco's Experience

Undisturbed, President Budeisky appealed for calm from players and spectators. He then requested that we turn on some car headlights and whatever lights were possible and point them towards the presentation area. After presenting the trophy to the USA, he requested that the USA team and their spectators sing their national anthem, which would normally have been played. This worked very well, marking the end of what was a memorable evening.

Sunday, June 11: Match Day 6 – Male Finals https://www.fih.hockey/events/hockey-5s-pan-am/schedule-fixtures-results

The USA and Trinidad put on an epic and memorable match for the finals. There had been little doubt as the competition proceeded about the possibility of both teams making the finals based on their respective dominance in the preliminary rounds. Again, Trinidad and Tobago looked the more dominant team but was outlasted by the USA in a competitively contested ebb and flow finals. These teams were already into the World Cup and were now just playing to see who would be crowned Number 1 from the Pan Am region.

Team Trinidad - Silver Medal

Team USA - Gold Medal

MVP - Marcano Teague

The Student versus the Teacher

But before we got to the final, and, with history on the line, it was time for the Student Coach Henlon, to compete against the Teacher Pablo Mendoza, for the bronze medal. Carlton and I watched the match from our VIP Bar overlooking the field above the Club House, trying to hide our nervousness. The Jamaican

Men's team had made the matches very interesting throughout the competition, especially the shootout with Guatemala in the crossover match and the 3:2 games with Puerto Rico. In both, they seemed to be in the ascendancy and then for some reason that the coaches and TD may be able to explain better, they made the result somewhat harder than needed based on their interesting decision making on the field.

This match would determine the final place on the Road to Oman for the first World Cup appearance for both countries. As we settled into the match, I uncomfortably watched the hunger and desire of the Jamaican Men for the final spot and they were leading at half time 3:0. It seemed we were in the driver's seat with smooth sailing to Oman.

Then the wheels came off the proverbial wagon, with a few cards (some a little bit questionable from my vantage point) for costly timeouts of the game, reducing Jamaica's playing numbers. Our unease came during a period of the game when Jamaica went down to two outfield players, George McGlashen and Richard Harris, and the Captain and Goalkeeper, Ajani Burton. For this period, Paraguay had their full complement of 5 players.

Ajani Burton in Action versus Paruguay

Ajani Burton was deservedly named Goalkeeper of the Tournament because what he did against the wave of attacks from Paraguay to deny them goals was nothing short of phenomenal.

Ajani Burton accepting his award at the closing ceremony
(Ajani Burton – PAHF)

It was probably providential that the two remaining players on the field were good defenders because defend they did, along with strong cheering support from the 6th team member – the supporters in the stands emphatically urging them to fight on in the critical period.

Richard Harris Overcome with Emotion Celebrating

George McGlashen in Action versus Paruguay (Gleaner Photo)

Booking the Ticket to Oman (Bronze Medal and History)

When parity was restored, Jamaica added the goals that sealed our ticket on the Road to Oman. Once the final whistle went, jubilation erupted, with scenes that had our security apparatus struggling to prevent the crowd from invading the field.

In the end, Nickoy Stephenson, a gifted and somewhat maturing but misunderstood player with an interesting personality, must be praised for his contribution to the Road to Oman. He was Jamaica's leading goal scorer and a big reason why we appeared in our first FIH World Cup.

Nickoy Stephenson and Coach Henlon

So the Student had defeated the Teacher, Dr. Holt's mentee, Coach Henlon, had outlasted Pablo Mendoza's squad to ensure another Caribbean representative at the H5s World Cup.

I made my way slowly down to the pitch, getting a few congratulations along the way, as our genuine hockey folks and supporters who had worked so hard over the past years, months and days fully understood what this victory meant for our program. I remember how, while joining the players and coaches on the field, Kameisha 'Polly' Erskine was so overjoyed that she took a shot of my rum and continued with the rivalry.

Overjoyed but composed, I tried to figure out how to help the technical team have Jamaica clear the respective playing areas for the finals. The single most memorable thing that happened for me on that field, in that moment, was an emotional hug from Christopher Reid, a player on the team, who said to me with tears in his eyes;

"Thank you President ... thank you ... You believed in us when all others doubted us ... You believe in the youths ... Thank you for believing."

That brought tears to my eyes as I recalled his youthful exuberance over the journey, dreaming to play at the highest level from a player who started in the Youth Development Program. I had to quickly engage my towel to maintain my composure. I still get emotional thinking about that moment as other players allowed me to join in their celebrations.

While other memories of the occasion are still a little blurry, I recall the raw emotion of Ebony McLean, the Manager with whom we had many fights, and our genuine hugs of joy. What topped off the moment was seeing the joy on Coach Henlon's face ... he was smiling for a change. Finally, my congratulatory hug with Dr. Holt who just kept on repeating, "World Cup bredda, World Cup ... I told you ... I told you so!" And yes, you did! ... History!

The Jamaica Gleaner Website

The Closing Ceremony

The distinguished Senior Common Room (SCR) crew, marshalled by Oshane Grant from The UWI Mona Campus, had come to support Team Jamaica from the vantage point of the VIP Bar (ensuring the spirits were kept high)[7]. A colleague and vibrant member from the SCR Crew, Meridian Kohler, indicated shortly after the closing ceremony that my voice sounded different from its usual deep timbre. In her words, I seemed to be slurring a bit. I suspect she was considering whether I was nervous or maybe having a medical crisis.

My laughter couldn't be contained in my response as she was correct. I replied with a smile, "I was and am exhausted!" However, I couldn't renege on my responsibility as President with so many people to thank, paying our respects to Captain Blake Roper, and ensuring I observed as many protocols as I could. And then, of course, I omitted from my list Mr. Noel Williams and the dedicated drivers from JUTA, as well as Dr. Rhonda Hutson and the dedicated volunteers from the Jamaica Association of Sports Medicine (dear Lord … this is why you write things down beforehand!).

Again, Marva Bernard, you were so correct ... This is hard but rewarding work! Addressing the closing ceremony was challenging, knowing full well all the work that was done, what was accomplished on a shoestring budget, and what we still needed to execute with logistics and payments before finally taking some much-needed rest. At least at this stage it was over!

I graciously accepted the PAHF award for hosting the event from President Budeisky. It meant a lot for me to accept the award on behalf of the many genuine, hard-working people in my functional/dysfunctional family. The hockey family sacrificed yet again and demonstrated that collectively, even on a shoestring budget and with lower levels of corporate support, we could host a memorable and historic event, the first ever Pan American Hockey5s World Cup Qualifier, here in Jamaica. It was indeed an accomplishment and, apparently, we were making it a habit to pull the rabbit out of the hat.

Award for Hosting Inaugural Pan Am Hockey5s World Cup Qualifiers

---

7 The SCR is a social club located on The UWI Mona Campus. It serves the Academic, Senior Administrative and Professional staff.

Another exciting and proud moment for me and certainly for the Jamaica hockey family and our well-wishers, was watching Jamaica accept the bronze medal that booked their place on the Road to Oman.

Being able to share the moment with Dr. Sharmella Roopchand-Martin and her husband, David Martin and their boys, Dylan and Shea Martin, made it more special. Apart from the role she played in developing the partnership with The UWI Mona Sports Academy, she was directly involved with the development and care of several of the athletes, especially those attending The UWI. Throughout the tournament, the Martins had shown their strong support of the Jamaican teams.

Team Jamaica Bronze Medal in 1st Hockey5s Pan Am World Cup Qualifier

The Hockey Field Is Now Silent

Bob Marley's son, Damion 'Junior Gong' Marley, has a song called "Affairs of the Heart". Although his sentiments were directed at a single female, with a stanza that goes "... when the tour bus drop off and all lights lock off and I'm a mere mortal again, promoter belly full and all the fans gone home, I am glad that you are more than a friend," I thought of the song and felt similar sentiments, sitting with a few friends and the ground crew at the deserted hockey field. It was amazing how quiet a stadium could get when everyone had left.

Our logistics was on point and all departures were successful, with no major hiccups. Dana's girls from Uruguay made their way to Montego Bay and so did a few officials and visitors. They were determined to enjoy the tremendous offerings of Jamaica, a jewel of an island.

Now that we had proved we were more than capable of reaching an international level competition, the Road to Oman must now be smooth ... it must be smooth sailing ...

It must be ...

... Finally landed in Dubai ... wow, a nice airport ... is this an airport or a giant expensive mall? A lovely food court with a variety of meals, but I'm a simple guy ... quick coffee and a donut ... darn ... these donuts are really sweet ... almost giving me a sugar rush at this time of the morning!

Summary

The Jamaica Men's team earned a bronze medal and booked their place in the inaugural qualifier for the region to their first FIH World Cup event. This they accomplished by defeating the Paraguay Men in a thrilling match from start to finish. The outstanding performance of Richard Harris, George McGlashen, and goalkeeper and Captain Ajani Burton were memorable, especially after the team was forced to play with three versus five while two players were penalized for a period of the game.

The tournament's quality was relatively high and competitive and provided an opportunity to view the emerging top PAHF teams within the region; that is, USA, TTO, JAM for the Men, and USA, Uruguay, and Paraguay for the Women. Despite finishing with silver medals, both Uruguay Women and TTO Men demonstrated high quality of play, and were rewarded with their placement at the World Cup Tournament.

It was interesting to see the student defeating the teacher, with Henlon versus Pablo for the bronze position of the Men. However, Pablo got the consolation of having the Paraguay Women defeat TTO for the bronze and a spot in the World Cup.

The experience of President Budeisky at the Women's closing ceremony when Kingston and St. Andrew had a blackout affecting the field provided another indication of his leadership skills.

Overall, the tournament and the bronze medal win solidified the JHF's strategic process, paradigm shift, and our investment in the Youth Development Program.

But we seemed to have read the tea leaves incorrectly, to assume that booking a place from the tournament meant an easy Road to Oman. It is now on to our unfortunate misreading of the situation and the management of the rocky road ahead in our journey to Oman.

Chapter Seven: The Rocky Road to Oman

Finally en route to Muscat ... Hello, can I sit here at the bulkhead? They are reserved for USD 110 if I want to move … What! In an empty plane! ... I am good! it isn't that long a flight anyway …

We had qualified for Oman. The hard work was done. Or was it? No surprise that it wasn't. It became an even rockier road once we knew we were heading for the World Cup. On this journey, we also had to plan, fund, and manage our CAC Games participation. Through it all, we had to face the many risks that sports leaders and administrators must handle to facilitate the performance of their sporting teams.

It was time to travel further on the Road to Oman, despite how much rockier it became.

The Pit Stop in the Dominican Republic enroute to Oman

Jamaica had a serious assignment in the Central American and Caribbean Games approximately two weeks after the Hockey5s Qualifier. This was being held in the Dominican Republic rather than in El Salvador because the original host (El Salvador) didn't have an official artificial pitch for hockey.

While the Men had automatically qualified by placing first in the qualification tournament in Bermuda, April 13–17, 2022, our Women had to wait and be given a promotion to a qualification spot based on the fact that El Salvador, now no longer hosting, had ceded the automatic qualification spot for females reserved for host countries. I think it was fortuitous as I felt our girls were very unlucky to have placed third in the qualifiers in Bermuda.

The NOC asked me to represent the Board in the Dominican Republic based on the number of athletes and coaches we had going on this tour from my Federation. We had a contingent of over 39 individuals for field hockey. Brandon Sealy and his coach, Tony Byon, were also in the Dominican Republic, competing in the Taekwondo competition. Brandon went on to earn a bronze medal.

Photo Op with Brandon Sealy and his coach

Earlier in my presidency, I had asked others to represent me as head of mission on assignments to various tournaments. However, I was not pleased with the inability to fully verify the reports returned on various issues, challenges, and performances. Therefore, based on the work that was being expended to finance the team's participation, it was necessary for me to see and observe the situation for myself.

I travelled with the team to Bermuda and was now going to the Dominican Republic. An irrefutable fact based on our budgetary constraints was the necessity for increased management experience and capabilities. This spanned negotiations as well as problem solving. Now, please understand, this is not an indictment on the management or coaching staff. It is simply the reality of working within federations to develop internal competence and people to share the responsibility.

Leading and managing people, including my beloved Jamaican people, across borders, especially athletes with various peculiarities, religious beliefs, dietary considerations and other social habits, is extremely difficult. Therefore, a major role that I had to play all the way to Oman was to try and ease the burden of the appointed manager and coaching staff in order to allow them to concentrate on the extensive requirements of the teams, especially given the budgetary constraints.

The difficulties and challenges handled in the Dominican Republic could fill a book. Let's just say it was fortuitous that I travelled with the delegation because various matters arose that needed immediate solution. For example, there was a lack of arrangements for athletes, communication challenges, transportation issues, or the need to purchase food for the team some 45 minutes away upon arrival at the village at approximately 11:30 p.m., and other immediate needs for pots, pans, a microwave, and utensils for the preparation of food. These challenges could not be explained without experiencing them firsthand.

Performance at the CAC Games

An extract from my Board report on the CAC Games:

"In summary, both teams advanced by placing 5th (Women) and 6th (Men) after qualifying via the CAC Games Qualifiers in Bermuda 2022. Based on the placement, both teams can concentrate directly on the next CAC Games rather than the cost associated with another CAC Qualifying event."

The Women's Team

The Men's Team CAC

Back on the Road to Oman

After returning from the long and exhausting trip to the Dominican Republic, it was time to focus on getting the necessary finances to have the team perform at an optimal level. "Did I read the tea leaves wrong?" We employed a similar strategy for raising funds and, in short, had issues and challenges. We continued to work the GoFundMe approach, knocked on corporate doors, spoke to the people who assisted in the past and made an extensive amount of media pleas but just came up short.

The well-laid out plans of Coach Henlon and Dr. Holt to fully prepare the Men for Oman were reshaped and reshaped, and reshaped again because we were unable to raise the required funds for practice matches and training camps, especially with stronger teams. We needed practice matches based on our performance at the qualifiers where some weaknesses were highlighted and plans made for correcting these before stepping onto the biggest stage of our hockey lives. The funding was just not coming.

Shocking News for the Journey to Oman

Still fighting to acquire funds and prepare the team as best as possible, we confidently submitted our budget to access government support based on our accomplishments. To my utter dismay and surprise, a response was provided, committing only 6% of our carefully crafted and submitted budget. To be fair, we received another 6% from the SDF but were significantly short of financing the budget for a world cup.

So, we had to go into overdrive to recast budgets, manage critical spending, and negotiate our way out of the situation, internally and externally, as there would be hell to pay if we didn't participate in the tournament.

Managing Crisis on the Road to Oman

As mentioned in Chapter 1, there may be some frayed relationships from our efforts to close the gap for funding the team to Oman. However, my thoughts were still positive as I couldn't imagine us knocking on the door of destiny and not being able to enter.

As we have shown thus far, sports administration and leadership in Jamaica are not for the faint of heart. Success requires serious leadership and management capabilities. In the period

---

8 https://www.instagram.com/reel/CtZOsl8Nsz1/?igsh=MWo2N2xvamtyd2o0bg%3D%3D

of crisis and the publicity of our challenges, we had to manage a fragile team of millennials and Gen Z-ers frustrated at how they could win a tournament, be congratulated by Prime Minister, Hon. Andrew Holness through his Instagram page on the accomplishment, and now worry about making the journey to the World Cup[8].

Screenshot of Prime Minister, Honourable Andrew Holness' Congratulatory Message to the Hockey5s Team on Securing Qualification to the Hockey5s World Cup

As mentioned in Chapter 5, under "The Difference of Gen X, Y and Z", an interesting blog post by Michael Mignano, a doctoral student, on the website of the Association for Applied Sports Psychology titled "Coaching Generation Z Athletes" provides a good context for the issues that we faced. Mignano highlighted factors similar to the ones we observed in Jamaica where our Gen Z athletes, while being fairly well informed via the use of technology, seem to have a much shorter attention span and need frequent (positive) reinforcement and feedback. They also seem to lack the independence to consistently train by themselves to accomplish improvement.

Mignano referenced the work of Gould and colleagues (2019) at the Institute for the Study of Youth Sports with the United States Tennis Association which focused on the advantages and challenges of working with Gen Z. The advantages included that they were motivated, educated, and strong visual learners with strong technology skills. However, similar to our observation in Jamaica, the disadvantages included the short attention span, poor in-person communication skills, lack of independence, perceived sense of entitlement, lack of gratitude, difficulty dealing with adversity, and complications relating to each other in their social network.

The withdrawal from the bid related to the T20 World Cup, which to a cricket-loving nation was unimaginable, had many awaiting similar bad news about the hockey team. This, based on our understanding of the psychology of the members of the team, particularly the Gen Z-ers, affected the final preparations of Team Jamaica for the tournament. We had to also manage what seemed to be delayed or not fully coordinated messages coming out of the Ministry of Sport.

Well, we are preparing to land in Muscat, Oman … I am getting this sneaky feeling about my checked bags. And to make matters worse, I didn't pack a full change of clothes in my carry-on as I normally do … But I am hoping for the best …

JHF needs $5m more to attend Hockey5s World Cup

Stewart: We have cut a lot of stuff after starting out with a $32-million budget. Airfare alone is $7 million and accommodation is $2-3 million. But a lot of the other things have been chopped ...

MONETARY COMMITMENT

STEWART

15 medals are within reach in Paris

Gleaner Article, "JHF needs $5m more to attend Hockey5s World Cup"

There was mounting pressure related to the financial requirements associated with the commitments required by FIH and Oman Hockey. Another area of pressure came from our own internal stakeholders and the pressing desire for the full resumption of local leagues and tournaments. The multidimensional pressures were tremendous.

Interestingly, as I did the media rounds to promote our sport's achievement, history, and the need to participate in Oman, I was calm about our prospects. This had nothing to do with understanding or having any contingency at this stage, but simply having worked through this type of crisis situation and having pulled the rabbit out of the hat on so many previous occasions. The need for a mature approach from the leader, supported by previous experiences, allowed us to operate and continue to execute the appropriate decisions on the changes to the critical way forward in a blink.

The support provided by Dr. Campbell, with his capacity to manage a successful business from the entrepreneurial stage to becoming a premier environmental consultancy in Jamaica and the Caribbean, 20 years later, was more than an asset at this crisis stage. Therefore, where others were unable to take particular types of financial and operational risks and decisions or to negotiate effectively, we remained steadfast and calm and continued to make the appropriate decisions for the Road to Oman.

Interview on Sportmaxx about JMD 3M shortfall

While we had faith in a positive outcome, we were aware of the possibility of a negative outcome and the serious effects that would have on the development of the sport ... especially when the news came that the committed funds would definitely not be transferred before our date of departure.

JOA to the Rescue

As identified in Chapter 1, President Christopher Samuda and the JOA were critical in paving the road for us to go to Oman. The JOA had been supporting the efforts of the JHF and monitored the development work that was done over the years and the resulting historical qualification for our first World Cup event. Therefore, when it was clear that we had a funding delay associated with the gaps we already had, it was the JOA to the rescue.

Jamaica Hockey Federation President Fabian Stewart (centre) presents a collage of photographs of members of the Hockey5s World Cup team to Jamaica Olympic Association (JOA) President Christopher Samuda (left) and General Secretary and CEO Ryan Foster. The JOA announced a $3 million funding for the national team to the Hockey5s World Cup. - Gleaner Staff Reporter Gregory Bryce

There may have been some who doubted the seriousness of our circumstances as outlined earlier because of our seemingly calm demeanor in the final days. However, had President Samuda and Ryan Foster of the JOA not assisted with their timely intervention, an approach the NOC had taken for other sporting bodies in crisis, our journey to Oman may have been halted.

Presentation from JHF to JOA

I can further assure readers that with that much-needed injection, our other critical financial shortfalls were tremendously aided by the generosity of our host, Dr. Marwan Al Juma, Chairman, and the Oman Hockey Association (OHA), and negotiations through the leadership of Tayyab Ikram, President of FIH, and his tremendous FIH team.

L-R Shakir Munir, Fabian, FIH President Tayyab Ikram and Ghulam Ghouls (GG)

Now with our accommodation secured and a requirement for visas to be issued (intransit ones for Turkey and visas for Oman), it was on to the negotiation of airfares, the reconciliation of team changes, and finalized bookings. Although breathing a sigh of relief, we were still mulling over the additional financial obligations for the comfort of the team, especially during travel. But we were now more confident than ever that the team would depart for its destiny in Oman.

Bags packed, I now played the role of the management forward team of one, departing approximately 48 hours before the team to finalize the necessary negotiations, some pending due to the delays in finalizing various payments.

This was indeed a rocky road as we seem to have hit a section that was less uneven but still not as smooth as we had hoped.

Top: Dr. Marwan Al Juma, Chairman OHA and Fabian

Bottom: View of the landscape preparing for landing in Muscat, Oman

Having narrowly avoided disaster, it was now time to concentrate on Jamaica's experience at top level international field hockey. Having no international warm-up games as per the technical staff's strong recommendation due to our financial constraints was definitely not the way we wished to enter top-flight hockey. The travel itinerary was also not as the coaches would have liked in order to allow for an earlier arrival to better acclimatize and possibly have some additional practice games. So, while Jamaica had earned its qualification, we entered Oman on a very rocky road, especially psychologically.

I landed in Muscat, Oman … wow … This has been a long journey … My dear Lord … thought tournament people would get special processing at immigration … man, this line is long and these guys are in no hurry at all … not at all …

Summary

Indeed, we misread the tea leaves regarding the difficulties associated with finalizing the journey to Oman. After qualifying for Oman, the Women's and Men's teams immediately set out for the CAC Games in the Dominican Republic, placing 5th and 6th respectively. Enough, we believed, for automatic qualification to the next CAC Games.

On return to Jamaica, it was quite clear that we had to pull another rabbit from the hat to get the team to participate in Oman and create history. Operating under consistent budgetary constraints, we as leaders, relying on professionalism, had to manage the situation with a high degree of emotional intelligence to reduce the psychological effects on the players and coaching staff.

Again, it was necessary to re-scope and make hard decisions such as not facilitating the required international pre-tournament warm up for the games requested by the coaching staff and reducing travel time before the tournament.

The tentative plans for the journey to Oman could only be solidified through the JOA's rescue mission. The JOA provided the requisite funds for accommodation in Oman, which allowed for the processing of visas and for other logistics to be completed.

We had made it to Oman. It was time for Jamaica to make history participating in its first World Cup event. But like all things, the international competitive environment promised no smoother road to an already rocky journey.

Chapter Eight:
Welcome to Muscat, Oman!

Yup, I knew it … I knew it … The turnstile is empty and no bag … Slow march to the Turkish Airlines Baggage Claim counter to find out where in the world my bag was currently located … I just knew it!

As a result of the delay on the Miami to Istanbul leg of my travel, I was rerouted by Turkish Air in Istanbul to Dubai and then on to Muscat, Oman. I arrived at approximately 4:30 a.m. After a few calls, a driver met me at the front of the airport and off we went to the Platinum Hotel. The ride was not long, with the driver pointing out magnificent mosques to me along our journey.

I had arrived, already relaying information to the team Jamaica contingent which was about to start their journey. Having pulled the rabbit out of the hat again, I was intent on enjoying and certainly absorbing this World Cup experience as best as possible. I recall saying to myself that regardless of any issues or challenges associated with our performance on this stage, I would not allow anyone to alter the feeling of accomplishment that I shared, and would share, with all the supporters and stakeholders that were responsible for getting us on the Road to Oman.

Welcome to Muscat

Entering the hotel that morning, I thought about the interesting direction in which the sun was rising. I tried to get oriented and settled as quickly as possible so I could begin to finalize various matters for the team.

Setting up my office

My body still was operating on Eastern Standard Time, so I was awake most nights while in Muscat. I tried to catch a few winks in the early morning (thank God for blackout curtains). So, it was logical for me to set up my virtual command center to operate at night.

It so happened that the best all-night Turkish coffee shop with the friendliest staff was located exactly beside the Platinum Hotel Oman where we all would be staying. I got to know their menu and staff members well, and communicated and handled management meetings extensively from the location, as the hotel's wi-fi could easily be accessed from the Coffee Shop. Shawarma, kebab, tea, Turkish coffee (strong stuff), and more tea (no alcohol ... bummer!) ... if you wanted a word with the President, you knew where to find me at 1 a.m. to 3 or 4 a.m.

Turkish Coffee Shop beside The Platinum Hotel

Having arrived before the official Jamaican contingent, I had to help myself, soliciting rides with friendly and not-so-familiar faces, such as the Uruguay field hockey team, to get around. On one such ride with the team, Juan Espasandín, President of Uruguay Hockey, reminded me that we didn't get to have a drink (Jamaican rum) while he was in Jamaica.

Rideshare with the Uruguay Team on our way to the Opening Ceremony
with Juan Espasandín waving to the camera

In my travels between the hotel and the hockey stadium where the matches were held, I was able to take in the geography of Muscat. As a student of Geography and of Geology, I was fascinated by the landscape and the developments within the environment. I think we have a lot to learn from Oman regarding building and developing for climate change.

The various minerals casting different colours from the carpholite-grade metamorphic rock is amazing. At first glance, one would think volcanic, but the high-pressure sedimentary formation gives rise to a landscape that seemed like a representation of biblical times.

The harsh-looking environment has a majestic beauty that creates a perfect backdrop to the Oman Hockey Stadium. The stadium, we learned, will be part of a massive sports complex which will also include a cricket pitch. The country is serious about sport, including field hockey development.

View from the Highway Running through the Mountains of the City and the Gulf of Oman

Oman's Culture

In the JHF thank you letter to Dr. Marwan Al Juma, I commented that despite the geographic distance and cultural differences, the excellent hospitality, food, accommodation and general friendliness of the people of Oman bore similarities with the Caribbean.

Laila our Liaison from the VIP Lounge
Left: with Michelle Right: with Fabian

Laila was a volunteer working in the business development VIP lounge as a liaison or host. She provided a practical and entertaining commentary on the culture of Oman. Her perspectives about the country, its religion, and its interest in tourism, particularly sports tourism, were insightful.

I recall Laila graciously offering to take Dr. Holt and I back to the hotel, for which we were grateful. In our numerous conversations, I would always comment on how clean Muscat appeared to be and not seeing litter or garbage on the roads. She would reply that a clean environment is mandated by the Koran and the citizens of Oman knew this. So, when I entered her car, I remarked, “Oh ... so this is where all the litter is kept!” We all laughed when she apologized and told us she hadn’t had the chance to clean her car from the start of the tournament as she had been so busy.

Laila mirrored the friendliness, kindness, and courtesy of most of the Omanians with whom we interacted. They were always willing to help and engage in conversation on any topic, including the Sultan, the history of Oman (the division and merger of sections of Oman), and adherence to Islam.

In fact, one of the noticeable scenes while in Oman was the preparation for and adherence to the call for prayer (Adhan) from the mosques, delivered five times per day as called by the Muezzin/Muadhin.

The Opening Ceremony

My early arrival also allowed me to attend the Hockey5s World Cup Opening Ceremony which was spectacular, with a beautiful light show preceding the official ceremony. It was unfortunate that the entire team was not able to experience this moment, but we simply didn't have the budget. This was a recurring theme, I realized, that affected a few other countries, especially teams that weren't participating in the women's draw of the tournament.

The Opening Ceremony

It was an extremely proud moment for me when the Jamaican flag was introduced on stage by a flag bearer. So, being the Jamaican contingent of one, I certainly let my voice be heard to the roar of the participants.

Women's Final, Netherlands vs India

Team Jamaica Arrives in Oman, January 25

Being the forward team of one to the Hockey5s World Cup, I arrived approximately 48 hours before the team. This was enough time to finalize the transportation to the hotel, especially with travel changes that occurred at the last minute. When Team Jamaica arrived at approximately 3 a.m. in the morning, they were expeditiously checked in at the hotel based on the arrangements I had finalized, and were ready for other business.

Team Jamaica arriving in Oman

Holy crap … Now my goalkeeper's and physio's bags have beer
in Istanbul. So I have to use my contacts from my experience ..
this number … call him ... and call him again … to expedi

Jamaica: Welcome to FIH International Hockey

Once the Jamaican men's team reached our destination on the Road to Oman, it was no secret that we were stepping into the ring with the 'big boys', who were more resourced and had investments in all sports, including field hockey, at a more serious level.

Some issues and challenges have come up with Team Jamaica … and that's why I am here … Let's work through them and learn together … Emotions are too high without the facts … Need some more coffee in "the office".

Our pool was packed with teams all above us in the international ranking, that is, Egypt, Switzerland, and India. They ranked in the top 40 of the world in outdoor and Hockey5s. They also have players extensively participating in international competitions regularly, as well as playing in European hockey leagues.

- https://www.fih.hockey/outdoor-hockey-rankings
- https://www.fih.hockey/hockey5s-rankings

It was now game time, despite the odds that were stacked against us. This led to one of the most memorable moments for me, our first match in an international FIH World Cup. The Jamaican

aica vs. Egypt Opening Game

national anthem was played alongside Egypt's and, in my mind, the moment concretized the work for National Team Excellence in our strategic plan, and signified more than six years of serious work to be able to stand on the field alongside those highly ranked international competitors.

Our flag fluttered in the on-and-off morning wind. This was the first time in history that Jamaica was participating in a FIH World Cup Event.

Dawn Staley, the head coach for the NCAA back-to-back champions, South Carolina Gamecocks women's basketball team, summed up my feelings about the World Cup Experience in a post-match interview (ESPN, 2024[9]). I recall her saying that this group of women were not supposed to be there (the finals and an unbeaten run of 39 and 0) after losing five of their starting players to the WNBA draft the year before. With tears running down her eyes and gathering herself she said, "... but once it's God's will, it is!"

This group of young men are by no means the most gifted or talented group of players that I have seen assembled in our sport over the years. This team was a combination or infusion of all the important elements discussed previously for successfully administering sports, including the improved practice of activities associated with leadership, strategic planning, coaching education, player development, and updated coaching methodology. Added to this was the shared vision and the right timing; it was simply a matter of "if Allah wills it," "إن شاء الله." In the case of this group, it was God's will at this time for Jamaica to take the Road to Oman to its first FIH World Cup.

---

9 Dawn Staley's Interview with ESPN, https://www.google.com/url?q=https://www.youtube.com/watch?v%3D6MeJG502u6U&sa=D&source=docs&ust=1725217342465915&usg=AOvVaw0RgvXdQCQLNiIxFRCIEzPE

The Men's Hockey Tournament, January 27–30, 2024

The final report on the FIH website provides a good summation of the quality of the final and the placement of the teams[10].

The Champion Netherland's Team11

It is interesting to note the final positions in the tournament where all the teams in our preliminary zone finished in the top 10 of the competition.

Table 2: Final Positions – Men's, Hockey5s World Cup 2024

1. Netherlands	9. Pakistan
2. Malaysia	10. Switzerland
3. Oman	11. Australia
4. Poland	12. New Zealand
5. India	13. USA
6. Egypt	14. Nigeria
7. Kenya	15. Fiji
8. Trinidad and Tobago	16. Jamaica

10 FIH. (January 31, 2024). "Netherlands crowned first ever men's FIH Hockey5s world champions as Oman clinch bronze." https://www.fih.hockey/events/hockey5s-worldcup-oman-2024/news/netherlands-crowned-first-ever-mens-fih-hockey5s-world-champions-as-oman-clinch-bronze.

11 Source: https://www.fih.hockey/events/hockey5s-worldcup-oman-2024/news/netherlands-crowned-first-ever-mens-fih-hockey5s-world-champions-as-oman-clinch-bronze.

Trinidad and Tobago had the best placement from the PAHF region, finishing 8th, demonstrating that the investment of our Caribbean neighbors in the sport is providing returns, especially in the smaller format of the game.

Somehow, I was cast into a role to make a presentation to the Pakistan team that had won the Challengers Trophy. The Challengers Trophy is for the top team that didn't make it to the quarter final round of the competition.

Unfortunately, I was not told this information before my arrival at the field, and as Murphy would have it, I had checked out of the hotel but left my jacket back at the hotel for a simple pick up and go after the Men's final, to return to Jamaica before the team, particularly to attend the funeral of the mother of Dave Lemard, my dear colleague, former Kingston College Old Boys (KCOB) Hockey Club captain, mentor, and friend.

As I was a bit hesitant to make the presentation in my usually bright Jamaican outfit, President Tayyhab Ikram first tried to find a jacket in my size (good luck with that). When that idea was not bearing fruit and I was prepared to offer my position to another colleague, President Ikram convincingly insisted that I had no choice in the matter. So I did, in a rather outstanding fashion.

Without a doubt, the quality of hockey at the tournament was exceedingly high and threatens to become much higher in the next iteration of the tournament. Top flight countries that either sent development or alternate senior teams for the smaller game, like the Australian development Men's team who were 10 seconds away from being beaten by Trinidad and Tobago in their 5:5 draw, and India's U21 Women's team that faced the Netherlands in the finals, or those who didn't participate, have already signalled a more serious interest in the Hockey5s format of the game.

Those teams and other no-shows will be vying more aggressively to play in the next World Cup Hockey5s based on the sheer excitement and success of this inaugural FIH event.

Coaches in Muscat, Oman

Jamaica Flag Flying Proudly, Muscat, Oman

Jamaica's Performance at the FIH Hockey5s World Cup (My Summary)

I stand by the excerpt provided by the media about our experience in Oman, despite not winning a single game. There was no way of learning what we learned, without travelling on the Road to Oman.

Excerpt from the *Jamaica Observer*, "Hockey Boss Sees Silver Lining"[12]

1. *Not the results we would have liked? But what do you think about the team's performance throughout the competition?*

Definitely not the results we wanted but a fair reflection of Hockey Jamaica's introduction to the international level of Global World Cup Hockey5. Having earned qualification over some 70 + countries worldwide, the result indicates that we are in the second tier (16th) at the world level for this growing format of the game. While obviously not pleased with our performance throughout the tournament, there were many significant positives for our team. However, the seemingly heavy mental weight of performance on the world stage, lack of experience with the speed and physical nature of the games, cultural differences, and other technicalities at the top flight level, created a very steep learning curve for our boys, especially without the required practice matches going into Oman. This affected how we could effectively sustain competitive periods within games ... which we had in parts against most all teams ... to score goals and not concede goals at the rate and phases of the game we did. Some of these issues can only be solved and corrected by more participation and practices at the international level.

2. *Have you seen any progress or development in the players?*

The players adapted to various aspects of the game and seemed to have garnered significant first-hand knowledge by competing with players only seen in international games online. The players and coaching staff are unanimous on the need for more games and tours at this level, similar to our Caribbean neighbours Trinidad & Tobago who finished in the top half of the tables, to see real progress.

---

12 Jamaica Observer. February 3, 2024, "Hockey boss sees silver lining after Jamaica's World Cup debut." Retrieved from: https://www.jamaicaobserver.com/2024/02/03/hockey-boss-sees-silver-lining-jamaicas-world-cup-debut/

3. *What's the feeling like, for Hockey Jamaica to participate in a World Cup?*

It was an unbelievable feeling to see the culmination of a strategic plan set in motion by the JHF Board in 2016, supported by the Minister of Sport, Hon. Babsy Grange, and SDF but, very importantly, the unwavering commitment of President Christopher Samuda [of the JOA] and General Secretary Ryan Foster who dared to believe in our ability to reach this international tournament and ensured our participation. So, my pride in watching the Jamaica flag flutter among 16 other international top-playing field hockey nations, can only be matched by my overwhelming desire to improve and cement our place at this level.

Summary

Participation in the World Cup was an experience that provided lessons for all participants on Team Jamaica. While Jamaica was allowed to complete various logistics and accommodation situations because of my early arrival, this was not ideal. The financial constraints played a major role in the sequence of activities related to Road to Oman. However, it is clear that the international level is different. Participating at this level and seriously contemplating top 10 and top 5 finishes will require an approach that expedites learning from the lessons that were offered to Team Jamaica at its first FIH World Cup.

Our participation illustrated that the Board of Directors continued unapologetically with the paradigm shift and redevelopment plans for what must be the basis of the renewed development pathways in our sport based on our experience and returns from investments.

At this juncture, the key takeaway is not the placement of the team. After all, we are ranked in the top 16 of teams in the world for Hockey5s. The takeaway is what it took to participate at the international competition level. Are we prepared to use these lessons to sustain Team Jamaica's participation at that level?

Sunset seen from the Crowne Plaza, Muscat Oman

Well, I need to get a few special things to pack and get set to leave … Oman was lovely … but I need some rum!

ROAD TO OMAN

LESSONS

Chapter Nine:
Lessons from the Road to Oman

As shared in the Introduction to this book, the intent was not only to provide a narrative on the history and journey of the Road to Oman but also to share lessons from the experiences. The hope is that the lessons may help other sports administrators and internal stakeholders to develop strategies for addressing complex problems and challenges faced in the sporting arena of small island nations and developing countries like Jamaica.

The journey to Oman was over but not the lessons learned. Here are the 14 lessons and recommendations this journey to Oman has left with this sports administrator and leader.

Presentation of Medal of Participation from FIH President, Tayyab to JHF President, Fabian Stewart

1. Invest in the process of strategic planning for sports administration

I think one of the fundamental lessons of the Road to Oman is the importance and need to engage in serious strategic planning for any organization. A good strategic plan will allow the organization to review the environment and its internal structure, and set clear objectives and KPIs for measurable deliverables for those objectives. This can be set against the budget or resource capabilities of the organization. It then allows the leaders to conduct evaluations, especially over the quadrennial, to assess the effectiveness of the organization's strategy in order to make adjustments.

The Strategic Plan developed for the Jamaica Hockey Federation in 2017 allowed for a clear, unequivocal understanding of the development priorities based on our limited financial resources and capabilities. It also allowed for changes to foster some development activities despite the unavoidable restrictions and challenges caused by the COVID-19 pandemic.

As outlined in Chapter 3, the strategic planning process had to be a priority based on the understanding of the complex environment and the distinctive and unique aspects of sports management:

- The marketing of the sport
- The financial structure or financial base
- Sports industry career path
- The enormous power and influence of sport as a social institution

The factors all dictate that an effective leader must develop and communicate goals that depend on aligned values with mutual benefits for its usually diverse stakeholders. This has to be done through a well-designed strategic planning process that is cognizant of the complexities.

Also mentioned in Chapter 3 was that a plan is simply a plan, and can be modified or changed based on the evaluation of the KPIs and changes in the environment. So, while the plans for participating in the Pan Am U21 tournament in 2020 and continued development of coaches under the Elite Coaching Programs were affected by the COVID-19 pandemic, an alternative virtual coaching program, involving smaller player group development, was executed. By quickly modifying the activities under the strategic objectives of National Team Excellence and Major Tournaments, the JHF kept focused and ultimately bid for and hosted the inaugural Hockey5s World Cup Qualifiers in Jamaica. We were able to do this because it was a smaller game, and we could therefore provide a facility and host the event. The performance of the team in qualification and infrastructure development can all be traced back through the strategic plans of the Federation.

2. A good leadership philosophy is imperative

Leadership is "an influence relationship aimed at moving organizations or groups towards an imagined future and depends upon alignment of values and establishment of mutual purpose" (Kane, 2014). As noted, there are many leadership theories, including the Great Man, Trait, and other behavioural theories such as Contingency (Fielder 1963) and Situational (Hersey and Blanchard 1970s). The Contingency and Situational theories informed the development of a difficult multidimensional leadership style akin to the Integrated Multi-Style approach (Hede, 2001) which I employed as President of the Federation.

The JHF, being a predominantly volunteer sport organization, has people of a range of personalities and capabilities, all of whom must be influenced towards a desired goal. The complexity in the organizational structure and the situational landscape of the Jamaican sporting arena was acknowledged. Therefore, leadership had to exhibit flexibility and adaptability in order to deliver. Many volunteers who occupied significant strategic positions had a lower than required maturity level or competence for the position. Therefore, rather than allowing the leader to follow or be directed by them (R1 or R2) to complete a task, he had to lead. This required more selling and telling concerning tasks (Situational Theory). The situation required a degree of supervision for various tasks to be completed and demanded a Leader/Manager multiple style (Hede, 2001), especially across the different organization segments and portfolios.

Although sometimes it is difficult to accomplish the multilayer leadership approach based on one's personality, it is necessary to effectively lead various sporting groups and organizations based on the situation. It is also important to understand the application and use of the varying styles of leadership. Therefore, understanding when to be autocratic, democratic, transformative or, when necessary, a servant leader, is crucial.

One could say there is a need for a certain level of fortitude to operate within the highly complex environment of a volunteer-based sporting federation or organization with many different stakeholder values, interests and skill levels. It requires courage in the face of situations of adversity and challenge (individual, operational, and financial). The focus on objectives must be clear so that, as a leader, consensus will not be sought at all times but clarity will be provided to the stakeholders. Results usually help to provide this clarity about an approach taken.

3. Sports Psychology (Focusing Gen X, Y and Z on the Real Objective)

It is important to realize that as a leader in sport, you are in fact working to serve a group of people – most of whom are predominantly volunteers – to accomplish a desired goal. In addition, in Jamaica and similar small island nations, most players, officials and administrators are part-time. This means a great level of sacrifice related to the delivery of service to the Federation or representation of the country. While the demands are high in the stressful environment of sports, it is important to understand and appreciate the differences in psychology and actions as outlined by our generational gaps; that is, Gen X, Gen Y (Millennial), Gen Z, and Gen Alpha. Therefore, the understanding and utilization of sport psychology and sport psychologists is important for successful outcomes.

A greater level of emotional intelligence and patience is required to operate in the region's sporting arena, particularly for non-traditional sports. To motivate and work on critical tasks with people displaying different attitudes across the generational profiles requires a keen level of emotional control and modified behavior, especially when handling players and coaches.

So, a leader has to consistently communicate clearly to everyone, especially using the strategic plan, in order to keep them focused on the agreed objectives (for example, winning games, qualifying for the Road to Oman) in a non-emotive manner. However, as I have come to learn, there has to be a mechanism or person (such as the sport psychologist) to assist with effective two-way communication in order to work through what could be distracting personal, technical and other challenges that could become major obstacles. This is simply because, despite a leader's perception of clarity, Gen X, Y, and Z's views on the treatment of various matters may not be fully aligned, leading to fractures in what was believed to be mutually agreed objectives and goals.

Jamaica Hockey5s Players, Coaches, and Management Team in Muscat, Oman

Jamaica Hockey5s Coaching Team in Muscat, Oman
L -R Yael Ragbir (physiotherapist), Kameisha 'Polly' Erskine - Assit. Coach, Devaughn Henlon Head Coach,Dr. Holt, Technical Director/Team Dr. and Ebony McLean Team Manager

4. Execute a Stakeholders Analysis

As mentioned in Chapter 3, it is very important to understand the value of people and their capabilities in managing a federation. This understanding comes from stakeholder analysis. While analyzing the internal and external stakeholders of the Federation, it was clear who were the influencers. This book has mentioned several internal stakeholders and their immense value to the Federation, based on their degree of competence and networking influence, both internal and external to the organization. Federations must develop and have a positive relationship with critical external stakeholders such as the government, NOCs and various corporate sponsors. This will allow for discussions concerning development plans, goals and resource requirements. A strong relationship will also allow a federation to understand the desired goals, values and interests of these stakeholders. This significantly aids in the negotiation of mutually beneficial agreements between the organizations and the federation, especially highly influential institutions.

5. Invest in youth players for the long term

Christopher Reid summed it up best when it comes to investing in our youth, following the team's bronze medal win at the Hockyey5s qualifiers:

"Thank you, President ... thank you ... You believed in us when all others doubted us ... you believe in the youths ... Thank you for believing."

Youth development programs must be taken seriously, especially in strategic planning. The introduction of new methods and technology, as well as game management information must be done early for greater adaptability and understanding. The same can be said for cross-border, regional, and possibly international competitions for the athletes.

Yes, small island states are going to have cyclical results in international competitiveness based on population size and size of player population. However, the consistent and continuous investment in youth players and programs will allow for less depressed or erratic cyclical downturns and gaps in national programs. This is logical based on the volume of potential selectees ready for competition at the higher level.

The investment in our youth players must extend to matriculation into continuing education programs, for instance through tertiary scholarships; that is, student athletic programs at various colleges and/or partnership exchange programs for educational and player development experiences internationally.

Young Shemar Gordon and Young Nickoy Stephenson are two youth players who matriculated to the senior national team.

Shemar Gordon

Nickoy Stephenson

6. Invest in technology for the game

The game has changed, and will continue to change at an incredible speed. Millennials and Gens Z and Alpha will not learn the game in the way Gen X and Boomers did. The athletes of today are different and wedded to technology for their development, information, and competitive edge. Therefore, to leapfrog in our development and close the current gaps or disparities in our sporting world, particularly for field hockey, we must invest in and use the requisite technology. We have to mandate the continuing education, especially related to technology, of our coaches and technical officials in order to become more competitive.

I had the opportunity to meet the data analysts from India and the Netherlands at the Hockey5s World Cup tournament. It was clear when I watched India play Jamaica that while there were noted technical differences at the player level, it was evident that the tactical difference was data-driven.

7. Focus on financial management

The management of finances, particularly budgeting, discussed in Chapter 3, is extremely important in any sports organization. The lessons associated with fully understanding the crafting of budgets, especially tournament budgets, can and should be reviewed in the *Advanced Sports Administration Manual* if we want to master the impact of proper financial management for our federation or organization. For us, the Road to Oman was built on the comprehension of financing, especially the critical budgetary exercise.

Most sport organizations will not have internal funding sources. Therefore, it's imperative that leaders know where to look and the process for securing external funding. Since field hockey, like many other sports, is an Olympic sport, understanding funding sources such as the Olympic Solidarity Program is key. The IOC is a non-profit organization and returns approximately 60% of its revenues to the athletes through the NOCs and IFs (https://olympics.com/ioc/funding). Sources such as Solidarity Funding are a major avenue providing funds to assist with the development of sports. For us, specifically designed and approved projects or programs for the development of our youth and coaching programs were supported by Olympic Solidarity Funding.

Another avenue for funding is corporate sponsorship. We understood, welcomed, and were extremely grateful for the support of our corporate donors. Despite lower than anticipated returns from corporate sponsorship for the Road to Oman, we appreciated the value. To facilitate this type of funding, it is critical to understand organizational core values, review the focus of their corporate foundations, and draft the sponsorship proposals to coincide with the focus or priority of the corporate organizations in a mutually beneficial manner. Doing so allows us to provide them with positive returns on their investment, partnership or association with our federation or organization.

The Best Dressed Chicken Sponsorship for 2022 CAC Games Qualifiers to Bermuda

The relationship with companies, particularly large corporations, must be carefully managed and nurtured based on the implications or ramifications of negative press that could be associated with the company's brand. Due to the nature of sports, various unsubstantiated emotional utterances are frequently overlooked at the local level. However, once corporate sponsorship is involved, there is the risk of serious reputational damage to the sponsor, unlike that which would affect a sports federation or association. Federations must develop various dynamic value-added benefits for corporations; for example, online takeovers and social media promotion (league promotion), as well as rebranding opportunities on facilities (that is, if the federation has management of its facility).

8. Develop and maintain relationships

The need to develop a wide range of sporting relationships cannot be overstated. It is inconceivable to advance on the international stage without local and international strategic alliances and partnerships. Our local partners, the Ministry of Sport and their sporting-related agencies, as well as the Jamaica Olympic Association are very important. Partnerships, such as the MOU signed with The UWI Mona Academy of Sport for advanced sport science training are advantageous, especially for elite athletic training.

The need to develop international and regional relationships was underscored by President Christopher Samuda, JOA, where, as a mentor in sports administration, he encouraged my understanding of the necessity to serve, if possible, on regional and/or international sporting bodies. Working and serving on the NOC and International Federation committees, panels, boards, or other IOC-related committees allows for a greater opportunity to understand the Olympic movement. This can lead to an individual's/federation's understanding of creating important arrangements that can be mutually beneficial for the institution and the country. In our case, one such example was the hosting of PAHF's first Regional Events Management Workshop, which assisted with the preparation for the Pan American Hockey5s World Cup Qualifiers.

Coco Budeisky, President PAHF, Fabian Stewart President JA, and Tayyab Ikram, President FIH

Eduardo Leonardo, Event Coordinator FIH and Fabian Stewart

9. Participate in international meetings and congresses

Regional and international meetings and congresses should be prioritized by administrators and leaders of sports organizations. The stakeholders of an organization have appointed or elected you to lead the organization by strategically aligning the goals and values of the stakeholders to be effective and, in the case of sports, competitive.

This means a leader must obtain as much knowledge from the international level of a sport to which the local body is affiliated to be able to properly guide and create a realistic vision and achievable mission for the organization and the people. Attendance at these conferences reinforces friendships, linkages, networking, and associations and, of course, helps develop and maintain relationships.

The FIH National Association Summit, Muscat, Oman, January 2024

10. Negotiate for technical assistance

For field hockey, there is no doubt that there is a disparity between the European federations and the other continental federations. At the Hockey5s World Cup, the Oman hockey team won the bronze medal. Poland was 4th, and both teams were Dutch-coached. It should be noted that the Dutch were also gold medal winners of both the Men's and Women's World Cup titles. Both teams were coached by a native of the Netherlands. The Netherlands' coaching pedigree and development capability in the technical area of field hockey is well-known and respected. They are also willing to share their knowledge. Therefore, for any sport or federation, certainly including the JHF, they need to tap into the capabilities of this European juggernaut in the sport.

This is not to deny the possibility of assistance from within our region. For example, Argentina has supported Hockey Jamaica tremendously over the past years. However, additional assistance from Europe could provide the impetus for continuing to narrow the gaps in our game at the international level. "To win, you must surround yourself with people who know or understand how to win!"

Fabian Stewart (President of JHF), Erik Klein Nagelvoort (President of Nederland Hockey) and Royston Hoggarth (England Executive Chairman Hockey)

11. Support and increase the cadre of international officials

This point is similar to the issue of serving at the highest level of the governing body of a sport. It is fundamental that if we want to have world-class players and teams, we must develop and maintain world-class officials. A perfect example of this is our Trinidad & Tobago neighbors, whose Ayanna McClean is an international FIH umpire participating in tournaments like the Olympics, Pro-leagues, Nations Cup and World Cup.

She was also voted FIH Umpire of the Year 2023. TTO was second in the Qualifiers but the highest-ranked Pan Am team in the Hockey5s World Cup at 8th. Having people officiating at the top level provides a synergy for the development of players who understand the latest rules and regulations of the game and their interpretation.

Ayanna McClean, T&T Hockey Umpire
Source: TTOC 2021 award feature address

12. Promote advanced sports management and leadership education

The investment in advanced sports management, sports project management and various leadership training offered by regional universities, such as The University of West Indies, Faculty of Sport, and the Jamaica Olympic Association (JOA) Solidarity Programs are necessities. These programs and courses provide appropriate information for the development of sports management team members for any federation or organization. They also assist with training volunteers, especially young people who may ultimately become part of the cadre of leaders in our organizations.

The fundamental understanding of topics critical to sports and project management will assist with the development and execution of programs and tasks that help the organization to gain competitive advantage in a complex environment with high levels of stress and varying stakeholder interests.

JOA Advanced Sports Management Course to the Diaspora article

13. Consistently aim for higher levels of competitiveness

One of the fundamental observations at the international level is that we have to work hard, build on any limited success, and keep progressively moving forward to consistently return to the international competitive arena. Teams can only gain the necessary experience at this level from repeated participation in international competitions. The paradigm shift for our sport needs to continue and we need to solidify and build on the development gains to lay the basis for further international participation and increased competitiveness.

This includes reviewing and making critical decisions to engage qualified professionals at the various levels of administration, management, international coaching, and technical officiating who are familiar with the requirements at that level. This will eliminate unforced errors and build on the strengths of a country, for example, our speed and athleticism, to gain the competitive advantage of our teams. If we can accomplish that, we can train and compete at a much higher level leading to repeat World Cup appearances in various formats of the game as the representative from the Caribbean, much like our neighbor, TTO.

Jamaican Flag flying in an international hockey competition

Attempts should be made to engage in discussion with the various funding holders to establish a partnership where, based on the experience of the Road to Oman, Jamaica is convinced that we are more than a two- or three-dimensional sports country. The Road to Oman should facilitate access to financial resources to create a realistic budgetary process to properly align the expected return and improved results from regional and international competitions in the sport of field hockey, much like our neighbor, Trinidad & Tobago.

While our Road to Oman was historic, it has to be looked at as an event and not a destination. We must believe we can entrench the desire to repeat and improve upon our strategies and actions to sustain all the facets that will support our reappearance at another World Cup event.

14. Enjoy the moments along the journey

We must find moments to ensure that we enjoy any returns for the hard work that we do to execute any project, most of all, navigating a World Cup appearance. This is of global significance. The moments are special and should be treated as monumental because they are, and may be once-in-a-lifetime experiences. This is despite negative criticisms, especially among the 25% of detractors. Issues and challenges should always be viewed as lessons, not just to be recorded but also corrected or resolved to ensure that they are mitigated as the project proceeds.

Finally, never forget to thank the special people along the journey, those who were in the trenches with you and those who made dreams like the Road to Oman a possibility.

Thank you players, friends, supporters, and well-wishers because you all travelled on the Road to Oman with us!

Fabian and Michelle

Conclusion

History is replete with special moments being explained through the prism of strong and adequate leadership and the unwavering strategy and commitment to achieving the desired outcomes. However, much of the significant events in history are a kaleidoscope of actions that are the outcome of unseen symbiotic activities that, at the appropriate time, forge a desired and memorable outcome and lessons.

The Road to Oman and the journey of Jamaica's Men's qualification to the country's first FIH World Cup Tournament since the sport's introduction to Jamaica by the military in 1902, was an outcome of fortuitous circumstances and work spanning over 8 years. The inaugural qualification was built on the foundation of actions and activities of key field hockey stalwarts and stakeholders such as Kitty Sharpe, Kay Wilson, Jasmine Campbell, Donald James, Colin Prince, Myrtle Weir, Stafford Shand, Stratton Palmer, Norris Davis, Kingsley Morris and many others who served the sport, demonstrating significant 'service above self'. The tremendous influences of these stalwarts, particularly those with whom I have interacted, underscores and entrenched the importance of the unselfish investments that have been and must be made in the youth development process for field hockey. It was understanding their contribution and work that allowed me to see the necessity to prioritize and focus on managing and investing in a new generation of younger stakeholders (coach, management and players). The return on investment was the qualification for and participation in the FIH World Cup in Oman in 2024 and qualification to the next CAC Games in the Dominican Republic in 2026.

The emotional journey to lead the Federation and ultimately the qualification to Jamaica's first FIH World Cup event provides many 'nuggets' or lessons that can be added to the literature about sports administration, particularly in small island nations such as Jamaica. I will never prescribe the highlighted lessons as exhaustive, or a fix-all to various sport administration challenges. However, the book incorporates a scholarly approach to include real-world practical scenarios and solutions along the Road to Oman. The scenarios included financial challenges, change management, partnership building, negotiations, dispute resolution, development prioritization and project planning, all important areas that provided insights for solutions and the important lessons.

The unwavering investment in youth, technology, and the coaching/technical officials cadre for the sport was clearly demonstrated with the levels of return on investment in the Federation's accomplishments under the National Teams Excellence pillar. However, it was also clear that the investments in the youth needed to be aligned with current sporting (coaching) education from recognized regional and international institutions to allow for current information to be transferred to our youth players to become more competitive.
Financial literacy, especially as it relates to the budgetary process, was covered and is absolutely necessary for the proper management of any federation or organization. This, coupled with intimate knowledge of how to access funding from sources such as Olympic Solidarity and negotiate for technical assistance, will be an asset to any development program.

Lessons from Malcom Gladwell's *Blink*, Mark Divine's *Staring Down the Wolf*, and Maxwell's *Leadershift* illustrated the building of a journey to lead the JHF and the approach to the decision-making process that ultimately crafted the Road to Oman. The reduction of fear and the use of 'thin slicing' allowed for greater freedom and expedited critical decisions. The approach also increased confidence in leadership, and saw the release from various productivity retarding constitutional committees and processes that were reducing the ability of the JHF's management to be effective in the current environment. Jamaica placed 16th at the FIH World Cup Hockey5s tournament in Oman, making the country rank 16th overall in the FIH World Ranking from a possible 86 countries that attempted qualification. It is, in fact, an adequate reflection of Jamaica based on the overall performance in the smaller format of the game and our various constraints. The historic qualification to the Hockey5s was based on the hard work of the coaching and management staff but, more importantly, the maturation of the Youth and Elite Coaching Programs.

Finally, one of the most important lessons from the Road to Oman, is simply, not to forget to enjoy every single moment along the journey. The world of sports administration, especially for leaders, can seem to be thankless if simply viewed as an empirical cost-benefit analysis of time (hours vs. opportunity costs), emotional investment, other resources exerted, and the types of psychological and other abuses that are possible because of decisions taken. Despite understanding the emotional and social impacts of sport on all stakeholders, especially in the proverbial 'fish bowl' (Foster, O'Reilly & Davila, 2016), it is important to have moments for celebrating the accomplishments along the way.

Having worked with a team to create a paradigm shift in our thinking and approach at the Federation, leading to Jamaica's first FIH field hockey World Cup appearance in the sport's 120 year history, the following quotes seem appropriate:

"In the middle of difficulty lies opportunity"
– Albert Einstein

"Rise above the storm and you will find the sunshine"
– Mario Fernandez

References

Allen, R. (June 11, 2023). Jamaica Men's Team Books Historic Spot to Hockey5s World Cup. Jamaica Observer. Retrieved June 18, 2024 from Https://Www.Jamaicaobserver.Com/2023/06/11/Jamaica-Mens-Team-Books-Historic-Spot-To-Hockey5s-World-Cup/.

Association for Applied Sport Psychology. (2007). Association for Applied Sport Psychology. http://appliedsportpsych.org/.

Bryce, G. (January 19, 2024). JOA to the rescue – Samuda: Muscat, Oman is not only a destination but destiny. The Gleaner. Retrieved on June 3, 2024 from https://jamaica-gleaner.com/article/sports/20240119/joa-rescue.

Camy, J., & Robinson, L. (Eds.). (2007). *Managing Olympic Sport Organizations* (Vol. 6). Champaign, IL: Human Kinetics.
Divine, M. (2020). *Staring Down the Wolf: 7 Leadership Commitments that Forge Elite Teams*. (First edition). St. Martin's Press.

Edigital. (2024). Different generation: Are generation names worldwide Edigital. Retrieved on August 1, 2024 from assurance. gov.gh. https://www.edigitalagency.com.au/market-research/best-generation-years-chart-names-list/.

ESPN [ESPN]. (April 7, 2024). Dawn Staley emotional after SC Gamescocks complete Perfect season|ESPN College Basketball, 2:40 sec. [Video]. YouTube. https://youtu.be/6MeJG502u6U?si=MJTynNB9wnmG3DW5.
Fédération International Hockey Academy. (2024). Coach Education: Coach the Athlete. Retrieved on June 16, 2024, from https://academy.fih.hockey/coach.

Foster, G., O'Reilly, N., & Davila, A. (2016). *Sport Business Management: Decision-making around the globe*. New York: Routledge.

Gladwell, M. (2005). *Blink: The Power of Thinking without Thinking*. Philadelphia, Pa.: Free Library of Philadelphia.

The Gleaner. (July 6, 2018). UWI Mona's Academy of Sport, JHF sign agreement to benefit athletes. Retrieved on June 3, 2024 from https://jamaica-gleaner.com/article/sports/20180706/uwi-monas-academy-sport-jhf-sign-agreement-benefit-athletes.

The Gleaner. (June 5, 2023). Rough starts for Jamaica at Hockey5s. Retrieved on June 8, 2024, from https://jamaica-gleaner.com/article/sports/20230605/rough-starts-jamaica-hockey5s.

Hede, Andrew. (2001). "Integrated Leadership: Multiple Styles for Maximal Effectiveness."
In: Parry, K.W. (Ed.) *Leadership in the Antipodes: Findings, Implications and a Leader Profile*. Wellington, NZ: Victoria University Institute of Policy Studies and the Centre for the Study of Leadership.

International Hockey Federation. (2004). Hockey5s: Pan American Cups #Jamaica2023 #5PCA202. Schedule And Results. Retrieved on June 3, 2024, from https://www.fih.hockey/events/hockey-5s-pan-am/schedule-fixtures-results

International Hockey Federation. (2004). Hockey 5s: World Cup Oman 2024. Retrieved on June 3, 2024, from https://www.fih.hockey/events/hockey5s-worldcup-oman-2024

International Hockey Federation. (2004). Outdoor Rankings. Retrieved on June 3, 2024, from https://www.fih.hockey/outdoor-hockey-rankings.

International Hockey Federation. (2004). Hockey5s Rankings. Retrieved on June 3, 2024, from Https://www.fih.hockey/hockey5s-rankings.

International Hockey Federation. (2009). Executive Board. FIH Board Members Tayyab Ikram, Maureen Craig Rousseau and Alberto 'Coco' Budeisky. Retrieved May 26, 2024 from https://www.fih.hockey/about-fih/executive-board.

Jamaica Observer. (February 3, 2024). Hockey boss sees silver lining after Jamaica's World Cup debut. Retrieved May 26, 2024, from https://www.jamaicaobserver.com/2024/02/03/hockey-boss-sees-silver-lining-jamaicas-world-cup-debut/.

Johnson, A. (2008). *The Brave May Fall but Never Yield: History of Kingston College, 1925–2006* (2nd ed). ISKAMOL.

Kerzner, H. (2017). *Project Management: A Systems Approach to Planning, Scheduling and Controlling* (12th ed.). New Jersey: Wiley & Sons Inc.

Larsen, E., & Gray, C. (2018). Project *Management: The Managerial Process*. New York: McGraw-Hill.

Masteralexis, L.P., Barr, C., & Hums, M. (2019). *Principles and Practices of Sport Management*. Burlington, Mass: Jones & Bartlett.

Maxwell, J.C. (2019). *Leadershift: The 11 Essential Changes Every Leader Must Embrace*. HarperCollins Leadership.

Mignano, M. (2019). Coaching Generation Z athletes. Association for Applied Sport Psychology. Retrieved on May 15, 2024, from https://appliedsportpsych.org/blog/2019/03/coaching-generation-z-athletes/

PlayerData, Inc (2024). Data for All. Retrieved on June 16, 2024 from https://www.playerdata.com/

Pan American Hockey Federation. (2023). Board Members. Retrieved on May 28, 2024 from https://www.panamhockey.org/pahf/board.

Panpatte, S., & Takale, V.D. (2019). To study the decision making process in an organization for its effectiveness. *International Journal of Business Management and Technology* 3(1), pp.73–78.

Pedersen, P.M., & Thibault, L. (2018). *Contemporary Sport Management with Web Study Guide* (Sixth edition). Human Kinetics.

Project Management Institute. (2017). *Guide to the Project Management Body of Knowledge* (PMBOK Guide) (Sixth Edition) and Agile Practice Guide (English). Project Management Institute.

Roopchand-Martin, S. (July 2, 2023). The story of hockey: Creating winners through partnerships in sport. The Gleaner. Retrieved on June 1, 2024, from https://jamaica-gleaner.com/article/sports/20230702/story-hockey.

Schermerhorn, J.R. (1997). Situational Leadership: Conversations with Paul Hersey. *Mid-American Journal of Business* 12(2). Retrieved on June 1, 2024, from https://citeseerx.ist.psu.edu/

About the Author

Fabian Stewart has more than 30 years' working experience across several sectors, particularly Information and Communications Technology (ICT), health care, building and construction, and the retail and the distributive trades. His expertise in business development, strategy and operational management was honed from various private consultancies and working engagements including JAMPRO, the Department of Foreign Affairs and International Trade (DFAIT) through the High Commission of Canada; the FIMI Group; New Era Homes 2000 Ltd; and The University of the West Indies (UWI), Mona, Business Development Office.

While the author remains an avid sportsman with diverse sporting interests, the introduction of field hockey at his alma mater, Kingston College High School for Boys in Jamaica, ignited the symbiotic growth in his education, professional and sporting careers. The author is recognized amongst the few to have represented their country at both the junior and senior levels while at high school.

While primarily working in the Business Development Office at The UWI Mona Campus, the author shared his wide spectrum of sporting administration knowledge as an Adjunct Lecturer for Sport Business Management and Sport Project Management in the Master of Science (MSc) Sports Business Management program.

The following highlights a few of his accomplishments and achievements including awards and merits:

- Board Member, Jamaica Olympic Association (JOA) – 2020–2025
- Board Member, Pan American Hockey Federation (PAHF) – 2021–2027
- President, Jamaica Hockey Federation – 2016–2024
- Fédération International Hockey (FIH) Medal of Participation for Jamaica Hockey5s World Cup, Muscat, Oman, 2024
- PAHF Award for Hosting the Pan American Hockey5s World Cup Qualifier, Jamaica 2023
- PAHF Youth Development Award – 2019
- PAHF Award for Hosting the Caribbean and Central America (CAC) Games Qualifier, Jamaica 2017
- Jamaica Youth Business Trust Mentor – 2014
- Co-founder of PHAT THURSDAYZ (Masters Hockey Group in Jamaica)
- Co-founder of the Revolution Hockey Club, 1995
- Coach, UWI Mona Campus Field Hockey Teams, 2009

- Locally Engaged Staff (LES) Meritorious Service Award from the High Commission of Canada, 2008
- Coaching Staff: Jamaica Women's National Hockey team 1996–99
- Captain (1998) Jamaica, Men's Hockey Team, CAC Games Caracas, Venezuela
- National Senior & Junior Field Hockey teams, 1987–98
- Games Committee Chairman, The UWI Mona Guild of Students, 1994–95
- Sports Man of the Year 1994/5 (1st Awardee as single sport for field hockey)
- UWI Team Captain, Mona Contingent (1995), Inter-Campus Games, St. Augustine, Trinidad & Tobago
- Player, Kingston College Old Boys (1986–1995)
- Coach/Player for Kingston College Old Boys (KCOB) Team 2000–2004
- Player/Captain, Kingston College High School (KC), 1983–1990

Tributes

Kay Wilson

I also thought how proud other foundation members would be of the accomplishment. One such foundation member was Mrs. Kay Wilson whom I had the privilege of meeting and interacting with in the early days of my presidency. While speaking to me about hockey at a coffee shop with her daughter Ruth Wilson in 2016, she mentioned her surprise when she saw some "young boy's picture in *The Gleaner* as the new JHF President", and I laughed and told her I was the 'young boy', to which we both had a hearty laugh. I also had a chance to visit her on the occasion of her 100th birthday.

Kay was a founding member of the Cecelio Hockey Club, the oldest hockey club in Jamaica. She had the distinction of being the longest serving president of the JWHA with her tenure spanning 1970–1979 and 1983–1986.

Her distinguished playing career commenced on a phenomenal note in 1956 when, on being capped for the first time, she was also appointed Team Manager to the inaugural Caribbean Triangular Tournament, held in Trinidad & Tobago. She went on to play and manage national teams of 1962, 1963 and 1964. At age 46, Kay ended her vintage national playing career and immediately donned her administrative hat. She plunged full-time into the business of sports administration, serving the Council as Honorary Treasurer and second Vice President, before being elected President in 1970.

Between 1970 and 1971, Kay focussed her efforts on acquiring the premises on Mona Road as the headquarters for the Association. It was not unusual to see Kay watering and weeding the field late at nights and early in the mornings. By 1977, 2 full hockey pitches were well-established on the property along with our very own clubhouse. This was no small feat as no other national association had its own grounds back then. Today, the property is still the centre for hockey in Jamaica and the headquarters of the Jamaica Hockey Federation (JHF), which was formed through an amalgamation of the former JWHA and the Jamaica Men's Hockey Association (JMHA).

The Jamaica hockey family thanks Kay for her unwavering optimism and her refusal to bow to the many detractors and obstacles along the way. She had a vision of what the JWHA could accomplish and dedicated herself to making this a reality. Her motto was "forward ever, backward never". Many of Kay's objectives for the JWHA were realized during her tenure, including bringing a number of international coaches to Jamaica and ensuring that both players and local coaches benefited from these visits. This, without a doubt, led to many fine performances of Jamaica Women's hockey teams over the years and the sharing of regional dominance for a long time with Trinidad & Tobago. While touring with national teams, Kay was always ready to participate in the fun and showed a great sense of humour even in the face of being the object of the team's mischievous pranks. She showed infinite patience even when confronted with flippant behavior by those she mentored, and continued to groom and encourage them, ensuring that the next generation of hockey administrators would have a solid foundation. Those who had the privilege of travelling with Mrs Wilson to congress, games or other such events watched her in action in absolute awe.

Mrs Wilson's tenure as an executive member, technical official and an administrator spanned not only local involvement but international as well. She distinguished herself in the technical field serving as delegate, juror of appeal and council member at many major international tournaments. A highlight of her career as a delegate of the International Federation of Women's Hockey Associations (IFWHA) was successfully bringing a motion to the International Council which resulted in South Africa being barred from all IFWHA and subsequent FIH tournaments due to their stance on apartheid.

The numerous links Kay forged and the respect that she earned on the international circuit secured a place of prominence for women's hockey in Jamaica among the international hockey fraternity. It is no wonder that in recognition of her knowledge of and dedication to sports administration she was called upon to serve on numerous local committees, boards and foundations such as the Carreras Sports Foundation (now RJR Sports Foundation), the Jamaica Olympic Association (JOA) and the G.C. Foster College of Physical Education & Sports, to name just a few.

In recognition of Kay's phenomenal service to the sport of hockey she was bestowed Honorary Life Member status of the Jamaica Women's Hockey Association on September 20, 1990. Kathleen, 'Kay', 'Willo', 'Wilson', was a pioneer, an icon, a strong, uncompromising, undaunted, determined, yet fun-loving woman who was forever open to new experiences. She especially loved touring and made many lifelong friends around the globe. She was a mixer, a militant, 'an international', and ultimately a mentor and role model for us. Forever a true champion of women in sports.

Colin Prince

Colin Prince gave voluntary service above self to the Jamaica Hockey Federation (JHF), its extended hockey family, as well as the Pan American Hockey Federation (PAHF) for over 40 years. He was a national junior representative, and a foundation member of the Circus Circle Hockey Team. However, he will be remembered best as an astute, stylish and confident umpire who exhibited exemplary performance at the local and international levels.

As a result of his consistent desire to improve and be amongst the best officials in the region, he was awarded his Federation of International Hockey (FIH) Grade 1 Umpire designation at the age of 29 years. His tenure as a Grade 1 umpire and subsequent international exposure allowed him to become one of Jamaica's most decorated and respected umpires regionally.

Based on his well-earned professional reputation, he officiated in some of the largest field hockey festivals and tournaments in the Pan American region. These included a number of Pan American Games (PANAM), Central American and Caribbean Games (CAC), regional games and Banks International Festivals in Barbados, until his retirement in 1998.

Colin Prince lived a life governed by high moral and ethical standards on and off the hockey pitch. He was always punctual, prepared and positive in his approach to tasks and challenges. It was easy to appreciate his objectivity and astute umpiring decisions based on his quiet, stoic demeanor and British-style wit. Colin's quiet confidence is best summed up by a quote from Mohammed Ali: "it's not bragging if you can back it up."

L-R Colin Prince, Valerie Hall, Myrna Brown (Life Member), Carol Hibbert and Carla Hewitt, Member of the Umpires and Technical Officials Group

Donald Hugh James

"An Iconic and a Once in a Generation Member of the Field Hockey Fraternity"